IMAGES
*of America*

# ANAHEIM
## 1940–2007

Charles A. Pearson, referred to by many as "Mr. Anaheim," served the Anaheim community for most of his life. Pearson, born in Ashland, Nebraska, on July 5, 1898, arrived in Anaheim in 1906. Active in local politics at an early age, he became the secretary of Anaheim's first planning commission in 1927. He was appointed to the Anaheim City Council on March 13, 1935, was elected mayor on April 15, 1940, and finally resigned in January 1959. Pearson was keenly aware of how adequate infrastructure permitted southland growth and campaigned for both water and energy programs most of his civic career. He worked personally with Walt Disney in 1954 to bring Disneyland to Anaheim. "Charlie," as he was affectionately known to most of the community, was often seen running his large basset hound, Beauregard, around Anaheim's City Park, just a short walk from his home. In recognition of his years of service to Anaheim and his 19 years as its mayor, the city council renamed the park in Pearson's honor on April 21, 1960. Few in Anaheim's 150-year history have contributed as much to its growth as did Charles Pearson.

ON THE COVER: Although Anaheim's farsighted leaders were already preparing for the city's growth, Disneyland's arrival in 1955 provided a catalyst for a transformation few thought possible. The 1950s would see the loss of the community's agricultural dominance, and by 1960, with the sevenfold increase in population to more than 104,000, the city would become "fastest growing city in America."

IMAGES
*of America*

# ANAHEIM
## 1940–2007

Stephen J. Faessel

ARCADIA
PUBLISHING

Published by Arcadia Publishing
Charleston SC, Chicago IL, Portsmouth NH, San Francisco CA

Library of Congress Catalog Card Number: 2006941039

For all general information contact Arcadia Publishing at:
Telephone 843-853-2070
Fax 843-853-0044
E-mail sales@arcadiapublishing.com
For customer service and orders:
Toll-Free 1-888-313-2665

Visit us on the Internet at www.arcadiapublishing.com

*Dedicated to the many families that have made Anaheim their home.*

Like almost 3,500 others that moved to Anaheim in the 1940s, the author's parents came searching for a new beginning and found it in the town of Anaheim. Norbert Faessel, a citrus broker by trade and a loving father by disposition, found that the little town with big aspirations held many opportunities for him as it did for his last child, Stephen (pictured). The author offers this work as his contribution to Anaheim's sesquicentennial celebration.

# CONTENTS

# ACKNOWLEDGMENTS

Again, my deepest appreciation goes to my supportive wife, Susan, for all of her effort in assisting in the selection of these photographs and captioning. I also cannot overlook my son Gregory, whose encouragement saw this work to its completion.

My most sincere thanks go to Jane Newell, local history curator of the Elizabeth Schultz History Room, Anaheim Public Library, for her more than generous assistance and support in the creation of this work. My thanks must also go to Ymelda Ventura and Sal Addotta, History Room staff members, who have been particularly helpful in providing the photograph and caption material required. Special thanks go to my close friend Opal Kissinger, who encouraged me to explore the history of a more modern Anaheim. Thank you, Dave, for your sportsmanship, Sheri for your plan, and Marcie for your enlightened guidance; for without you all, this might not have been completed.

Photograph credit goes to the Anaheim Public Library's Digital Anaheim Project, which has made more than 2,000 vintage Anaheim images available to the residents, scholars, and historians throughout the world. Additional photograph credit must go to the City of Anaheim Community Development (Elisa Stipkovich, executive director); City of Anaheim External Affairs Office (John Nicolletti, manager); Steve Swain, Community Services superintendent; and Phil Brigandi, archivist at the Orange County Archives, who is a true historian in his own right and one that I greatly admire.

In writing the captions, the work of the late Dr. Leo J. Friis, Anaheim's historian laureate, John Westcott (*Anaheim: City of Dreams*), Geoff Black, Bret Colson (*Dreams to Reality, a Profile of Modern Day Anaheim*), and this author's earlier work were relied upon. Not to be overlooked were the Norbert Faessel family that arrived in Anaheim in 1942 and the Ralph Warden family that located here in 1960, like so many others that were searching for a new beginning and found it in Anaheim. Through the efforts of the Anaheim Mother Colony Household, Inc. (Harold Bastrup, president emeritus), the Anaheim Historical Society, Inc. (Cynthia Ward, president), and the Anaheim Museum, Inc. (Joyce Franklin, exhibits director), Anaheim's unique history will not be forgotten.

# INTRODUCTION

Since its founding 150 years ago, Anaheim has repeatedly survived natural and man-made disasters to become California's 10th largest city, an international tourist destination, and the center for sports and entertainment in Southern California. Often called the "City of Dreams" for the ability of its leaders to take a dream and turn it into reality, Anaheim's passage from a citrus-centered economy in 1940 to its tourist-, entertainment-, and industrial-driven economy of the 21st century clearly shows Anaheim's "can-do" spirit.

This path to growth, however, was not accidental. As the county's oldest community, Anaheim had leaders who promoted the area in the 1920s through the California Valencia Orange Show, where they boosted not only the area's most important crop, but also the community as a good place to live and work. City leaders realized early that the dependence on agriculture would hinder the area's growth, and this prompted a number of local businessmen to create the Anaheim Industrial Land Development Company in 1924. This privately funded firm offered potential companies land below market rates as an inducement to settle in Anaheim. With the creation of the first Planning Commission in Orange County in 1927, Anaheim would ensure that it would be the leader in commercial and residential growth as it approached mid-century.

The city made early commitments to long-term infrastructure improvements that would later make residential and commercial growth possible. The connection to a regional sanitary sewer system in the 1910s and a much bolder step to join the Metropolitan Water District of Southern California in 1928 and tap the Colorado River 300 miles away would together assure Anaheim potential growth well into the late 20th century.

Just as the grape blight of the 1880s forced the German settlers to find another profitable crop for their livelihood, so did another act of nature in the late 1940s trigger a significant change in the area's land use. A citrus virus (citrus tristeza *closterovirus*) simply called "Quick Decline" would devastate the region's Valencia orange crop. The accelerating loss of this agricultural industry, coupled with the new higher cost of irrigation water, gave the citrus ranchers a strong incentive to sell their land for residential development.

The area's mild Mediterranean-like climate, earlier touted by the citrus-driven chamber of commerce as the "frostless belt," now attracted many returning World War II veterans who found the local weather, moderate housing prices, and job opportunities desirable. Southern California was the land of opportunity in the postwar era, and the growth of Anaheim and greater Orange County would later be phenomenal.

This growth would lead Hollywood animator Walt Disney to the Anaheim area in the fall of 1953 in search of a site for his new amusement park. Walt Disney's 20-year dream of establishing a new concept park where both adults and children could enjoy themselves brought him to where the Stanford Research Institute claimed the center of southland growth would be, just a short distance south of the Anaheim city limits.

Soon the 160 acres of oranges and walnuts located along South Harbor Boulevard would be changed into the "Happiest Place on Earth," and along with Walt's Sunday night television show,

Disneyland would overnight propel the name Anaheim into the collective memory of every family in America. Again Anaheim's "can do" spirit took care of the many requirements posed by Disney—from annexing the 768 acres surrounding the future park and closing a little-used road that crossed the property to ensuring that the signature address of 1313 South Harbor Boulevard could be used. Disneyland's opening day on July 17, 1955, was a nationally televised event, and almost overnight, Anaheim became a new family vacation destination.

Anaheim's business-friendly climate allowed unexpected rapid and unplanned growth around the Disneyland park area in the 1960s and 1970s, an issue that city leaders would need to address as the 21st century neared.

Disneyland was often just a summer family destination, and to encourage the yearlong use of the park and the many hotel rooms surrounding it, Anaheim leaders proposed the construction of a convention center. This concept, around Anaheim business circles since the 1930s, finally saw its realization when ground was broken in a cleared orange grove in typical Anaheim fashion—a dynamite explosion. The $14.5 million Anaheim Convention Center, which opened in 1967, is, after several expansions, today the largest facility of its type on the West Coast and one of the largest centers in the country.

In 1964, leaders, recalling the 1940s when Connie Mack's Philadelphia Athletics called Anaheim home for their spring training, acted decisively to attract Gene Autry's Los Angeles Angels to Anaheim. The city closed the deal with Autry and fast-tracked the construction of the new $15.8 million Anaheim Stadium in order to make an April 9, 1966, deadline for an exhibition game.

Anaheim's population swelled from 14,522 in 1950 to more than 104,000 within the decade, putting major strains on the city services. In the 1960s, the community supported new civic facilities such as libraries, new police and additional fire stations, infrastructure improvements, and later a new city hall. Growth in the Orange County area also brought with it new regional shopping centers that drew customers away from Anaheim's downtown businesses, leading to a downward spiral that would culminate in urban redevelopment and the eventual loss of Anaheim's beloved old business center in the late 1970s.

Anaheim residential growth was often driven by its aggressive annexation program, adding 20 square miles in the 1950s alone. Anaheim's sphere of influence crossed the Santa Ana River in the 1960s, cementing Anaheim's stake in the Santa Ana Canyon. In 1970, the 4,200-acre, upscale planned community of Anaheim Hills was born, soon followed by additional developments that would boast a population in the hills of more than 65,000 by 2002.

As Anaheim reached its sesquicentennial year of 2007, new urban style development is becoming a reality around the Anaheim Stadium area. Now called the Platinum Triangle, this area will see thousands of new residential units, shopping, and additional entertainment opportunities. Long-awaited development in the downtown area will include additional housing units and much needed cultural arts venues and finally complete the decades-old vision of a new downtown. The growth anticipated by Anaheim's early leaders almost 80 years ago has indeed arrived, and there seems to be no pause in sight, truly fulfilling Anaheim's motto of "Where the world comes to live, work, and play."

# One

# 1940–1949
## "The Capital of the Valencia Orange Empire"

The late-ripening Valencia orange was well suited for Anaheim's mild climate (often touted as the "frostless belt") and well-drained soil. As the most successful replacement for the loss of Anaheim's grape industry due to blight in the 1880s, which killed almost every vine in the region, citriculture gave Anaheim, as well as most of the region, a thriving economy. Every rancher would still listen for Floyd Young's 8:00 p.m. Fruit Frost Report on KFI radio, as the local orange crop was more important than national news. By 1938, the peak of the Valencia orange in Orange County, 67,536 acres were planted with production of more than 9.3 million boxes of oranges, worth almost $17 million.

Anaheim was home to a number of regional packinghouses. The town was a dominant producer of the Valencia orange in the first half of the 20th century, packing over five million boxes by 1930. The interior of the Orange Belt Fruit Distributors, located at 805 East Center Street (now Lincoln Avenue), is seen in this c. 1940 view. Local women worked seasonally for the firms and handled the actual grading and packing of the fruit in this era. Pictured here are, from left to right, Marcella Gomez, Chonita Veyna, and two unidentified women packing Orange Belt's Three Star brand of locally grown fruit.

The Anaheim Cooperative Orange Association was one of a number of packinghouses owned by the growers themselves, which allowed the citrus rancher the opportunity to have control of packing and marketing functions. The association's modern facility was located at 1530–1540 West Lincoln Avenue. In this 1943 view, Charles Reynolds prepares crates of the co-op's Autumn Leaf brand for shipment via rail.

Most of Anaheim's orange packinghouses were built adjacent to one of the area's rail lines. On the west side of Anaheim, a number of facilities hugged the Santa Fe Railway mainline. Frank Belmont's modern Granada Packing House is located just left of center, with Borden Fruit Company, Orange Belt Fruit Distributors, and Webb Packing all facing East Center Street (now Lincoln Avenue) at far right. Anaheim's 1923 Union Pacific Depot is seen at lower right as are Anaheim's landmark twin 200-foot-long natural gas tanks on Topeka Street.

Looking east in this aerial view across Atchison Street between Center Street (now Lincoln Avenue) and Broadway shows the newly built 1941 Santa Fe Depot at upper left, the Borden Fruit Company and the Anaheim Citrus Fruit Association across the tracks, and the juice processor, E. A. Silzle, at the street corner, right of center in the photograph. Union Pacific Railroad's turntable at the end of their Anaheim Branch line is seen at lower right. The many orange groves that supplied these firms can still be seen in the distance.

11

THORNROSE PHOTO CO. 1948

LA PALMA PARK
ANAHEIM, CALIF N 15

Anaheim leaders began discussing a second public park in 1935. An unkempt lot at the north entrance of town was acquired through a land swap for part of the city's orange grove on its old sewer farm on Loara Street. The new name of La Palma Park was chosen by a public lottery. After several years of delays, including the flood of March 3, 1938, which ruined most of the work accomplished to that date, the park was dedicated on Saturday, August 4, 1939. One of the first uses for the park's hardball diamond and concrete bleachers was as spring training grounds for a number of Pacific Coast AAA teams, including the Los Angeles Angels in the 1943, 1944, and 1945 seasons and the St. Louis Browns in 1946.

Professional baseball finally arrived in Anaheim when Connie Mack brought his Philadelphia Athletics to town in the spring of 1940. Mack, part owner of the team and a Hall of Fame member, was a very popular and accessible personality during the time his players practiced in the palm tree–ringed baseball diamond. His team would live at both the Pickwick and Angelina Hotels while in town and would stop by the Elk's Club for meals. The Athletics would practice in Anaheim through the 1943 season, when wartime travel restrictions ended their annual visit. The St. Louis Browns would also practice in Anaheim during the 1946 season. Here Connie Mack discusses the finer points of the game to a group of local young fans.

Vic Ruedy, La Palma Park's groundsman and a past professional baseball player, would keep the full-sized hardball field in tip-top shape for the players. Anaheim, long a baseball town that fielded a number of business and fraternal teams over the years, strongly supported the professional teams who, if only briefly, called Anaheim home. This 1940 scene from an exhibition game at the park shows Anaheim police chief James S. Bouldin trying his luck in the batter's box. Twenty-four years later, Vic Ruedy would be called out of retirement to help plan the field for a Los Angeles team owned by a singing cowboy that would soon be relocating to Anaheim.

The extensive use of water-well drilling gave the local citrus rancher an almost unlimited supply of irrigation water. By 1913, subsurface water levels had dropped over 50 feet and continued to fall, rendering many wells, including one municipal one, useless. Anaheim, along with other southland communities, realized a distant water source would be required to ensure the region's future growth. Anaheim became one of the original "Thirteen Golden Cities" that created the Metropolitan Water District of Southern California in 1928. Over 10 years of construction was required to bring the Colorado River to Anaheim taps. This photograph shows the construction of Anaheim's first aqueduct connection at the corner of East Center Street (now Lincoln Avenue) and East Street.

Anaheim's Municipal Water and Light superintendent, Vard "Pappy" Hannum, had his "boys" install a new 12-inch water main along East Center Street (now Lincoln Avenue) in 1941 to connect with the aqueduct's Orange County feeder at East Street. Although rarely used in the World War II era, this new water source became extremely valuable in the postwar years as residential and commercial development far exceeded the capacity of the region's underground aquifer.

Most of Anaheim survived the World War II years well, although a number of its sons and daughters were lost to the conflict. Also affected were the area's many residents of Japanese ancestry, who were relocated by President Roosevelt's Executive Order 9066. Anaheim had a significant number of Japanese who maintained businesses or ran small truck farms. Many of these industrious, patriotic families lost almost everything when required to move and sit out the war in internment camps.

WESTERN DEFENSE COMMAND AND FOURTH ARMY
WARTIME CIVIL CONTROL ADMINISTRATION
Presidio of San Francisco, California
May 10, 1942

# INSTRUCTIONS
## TO ALL PERSONS OF
# JAPANESE
## ANCESTRY
### Living in the Following Area:

To protect the families at home, an air raid tower was built behind the city's powerhouse on Claudina Street. Here two-person "warden" teams (and often one helper) would watch the night sky for danger. Every flying object was noted, recorded, and regularly phoned in to local command. A young James J. Friis recalls the harrowing climb up the wooden stairs to assist on several dark nights. (Photograph by Betzsold; courtesy of Brad Pettigrew.)

15

Carl Karcher, a farmer's son from Ohio, was employed by the Armstrong Bakery in Los Angeles and delivered bread to stores in the area. On July 17, 1941, Carl and his wife, Margaret, borrowed $311 on their Plymouth and with $15 in savings purchased a hot dog cart at the corner of Florence and Central Streets in Los Angeles. In a short while, the couple owned four successful carts and on January 16, 1945, opened their first family restaurant, Carl's Drive-In Barbeque, in Anaheim at 1108 North Palm Street (now Harbor Boulevard). Fueled by the postwar Orange County residential boom, Carl and Margaret would look to further expand their business. (Courtesy of CKE Restaurants, Inc. Archives.)

Karcher's combination of hard work, strong faith, and a keen knowledge of the eating habits of postwar America encouraged him to open a smaller version of his full-service restaurant in 1956. The first Carl's Jr. opened at the corner of West Center Street (now Lincoln Avenue) and Janss Street, located between Anaheim High School, Fremont Junior High, and his children's school, St. Boniface. By 2007, more than 1,000 Carl's Jr. locations operated nationally. Carl and his wife, Margaret, would receive their Anaheim Walk of Stars recognition in early 2007. (Courtesy of CKE Restaurants, Inc. Archives.)

Victor G. Loly, an Englishman, arrived in the southland in 1912 and became engaged in the jewelry business. With the advent of World War I, he was one of the first from Anaheim to enlist in the service and, upon his return, reentered the jewelry business. In May 1946, he relocated to this new modern showroom at 138 West Center Street (now Lincoln Avenue). The new store featured modern furnishings that highlighted Loly's exquisite inventory of fine jewelry and silver, and his unique animated window displays from the Baringer Display Company always attracted attention. Considered one of the premier jewelers in the region, he often was visited by Hollywood's elite, as well as many of his own friends in Anaheim. Loly is pictured at center flanked by his staff. Sadly, after Victor's death in 1963 and the deteriorating business conditions in downtown Anaheim, this signature business closed in 1969. (Courtesy of Victoria Loly Little.)

After World War II, local businessman Cortez Hoskins began to develop a small tract just north of Anaheim's City Park. Palm Street (now Harbor Boulevard) is seen at the bottom of the photograph with Sycamore Street visible at the right. Hoskins would name one of the new streets Leonora in loving recognition of his wife. By summer 1946, only the Hoskins, Marion Henry, and John Ganahl homes are constructed.

This 1946 view of central Anaheim shows its proud 20-acre City Park. After many years of disputes and two unsuccessful trips to the polls, the funds required to buy the land were finally approved in 1920 by Anaheim voters, and one of the town's most ambitious projects was later constructed. City Park included picnic grounds, a lighted softball field, a heated Olympic-sized plunge, goldfish-filled lagoons, tennis courts, and an open-air theater that could seat 2,000. Anaheim would become known as the "City with the Beautiful Park."

18

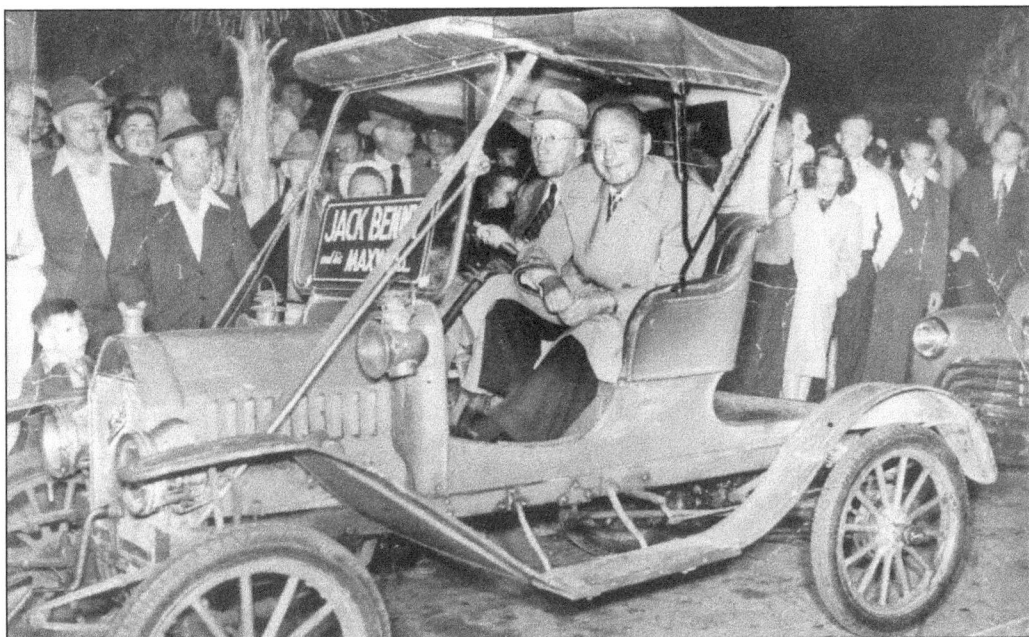

Jack Benny was the nation's most popular radio comedian when, on Sunday evening, January 7, 1945, he included the name of the town in his famous "Train leaving on track 5 for Anaheim, Azusa and Cuc–amonga!" comedy skit. The Anaheim Chamber of Commerce rushed to "adopt" Benny as its own native son, and plans were eventually finalized to have "Mr. Sunday Night" himself visit Anaheim during its inaugural Civic Progress Week celebration on April 21, 1947. The star arrived at the Elk's clubhouse on North Los Angeles Street (now Anaheim Boulevard) in a 1906 Maxwell driven by local Superior Court judge Raymond Thompson. This view shows Benny's arrival for the evening show surrounded by most of the community, including six-year-old David Faessel, who is surprised to see the famous radio voice in person.

Benny entertained the lucky 340 who received tickets for the banquet at the Elks Club with a comedy routine, his signature "Love in Bloom" violin solo, and also by introducing the new Miss Anaheim, Phyllis Officer, to the appreciative crowd. The highlight of the evening was Benny (left) being presented an inscribed gavel as "Honorary Mayor" of Anaheim by Mayor Charles Pearson. Jack promised to "try it out by driving 80 miles per hour out of town!"

Anaheim's entrepreneurial German Trustees had begun the City Water Department in 1879 and their own electric utility in 1894. On December 30, 1946, this portrait of Anaheim's Municipal Light Water and Power was taken in front of the town's 1907 powerhouse at 518 South Los Angeles Street (now Anaheim Boulevard). Pictured here are, from left to right, (first row) Bill Hedrick, Frank Sackett, Gus Lenain, John Thornhill, George Oelkers, Vernon Wright, Vard Hannum, Joe Schultz, Fred Cordonnier, Cameron Miller, Ernest Nichols, and Max Moody; (second row) Jim Cottle, Phil Schrott, George Nelson, Tony Hund, Bill Fry, Clyde Reist, Jim Betzhold, George Smith, Joe Garcia, Louis "Tillie" LaSaout, Lou Schrott, Oren Morey, Andrew Cooper, and Vanus Aiken.

This 1947 aerial view shows north Anaheim's industrial area, bordered by North Lemon Street to the west, Commercial Street to the north, the Santa Fe Railway to the east, and La Palma Street to the south. The town's first manufacturing firms were located here. In 1924, realizing that Anaheim's dependence on only agriculture would inhibit its growth, a group of businessmen created the Anaheim Industrial Land Development Company. This privately funded organization would offer land to prospective manufacturing firms at rates well below market value as an incentive to locate in Anaheim. By 1947, U.S. Industrial Chemicals, Inc. (industrial alcohol), Essex Wire Corporation (electrical wire), General Electric (synthetic resins), Southern California Citrus Foods (citrus by-products), Bridgford Company (meat packers), and Rinshed-Mason Company (automotive paint) had located here.

By 1948, Anaheim's population was approaching 14,000 with the arrival of many postwar veterans who found the region's climate, moderate housing prices, and jobs attractive. The town's dependence upon its citriculture heritage was still significant but waning as a new citrus disease called "Quick Decline" was beginning to ravage the local groves. Anaheim's downtown was still a magnet for the shoppers as this view looking east on Center Street (now Lincoln Avenue) shows. The county's tallest structure, the six-story Kraemer Building, is seen in the distance.

By the late 1940s, Anaheim was already beginning to grow beyond its historical North, South, East, and West Streets boundaries. Significant annexation beginning in 1944 would increase the city's area by 25 percent by 1950. Orange groves surrounding the town can still be seen in this late-1940s view, but the peak of local Valencia orange production had passed and residential development was now the talk on the street. This aerial view is looking northeast with Center Street (now Lincoln Avenue) seen diagonally from lower left to upper right.

The Anaheim Chamber of Commerce, in cooperation with the Planning Commission and a number of local businesses, presented a second Civic Progress Week celebration in May 1948. A vacant lot at the southwest corner of La Palma and North Palm Street (now Harbor Boulevard) was converted into fairgrounds that featured a 26,000-square-foot tent where local business opportunities could be promoted as well as a sideshow that included 9¢ carnival rides for children and adults. The 1947 Civic Progress Week featured an address by Walter Elieson, deputy director of the U.S. Commerce Department, who was prophetically quoted: "You haven't begun to see the growth that is coming your way." Anaheim's continued boosting of the community would, in the next decade, bring growth well beyond even Elieson's expectations.

Anaheim's 1947 Halloween parade is pictured in front of the Fox Theater at 229 West Center Street. The children in costume, riding the wagon pulled by a "witch," are illustrating the story of *Hansel and Gretel*. Anaheim's old California Theater was converted to the Fox, and the new lighted marquee advertises a double feature starring Rex Harrison and Maureen O'Hara.

In 1949, Agnes Francis Criss, who had taught in both public and private business colleges, opened the Criss Business College at 512 East Center Street (now Lincoln Avenue). This coeducational school taught male and female students the skills required to be successful in future business careers. Emphasis was placed on typing, shorthand, and bookkeeping skills. Pictured here outside the school on Center Street are Virginia Criss (left) and her cousin Marjorie Criss.

One of Anaheim's most important postwar industries was Kwikset Locks, which located to the corner of Olive and Santa Ana Streets in 1948. Inventor Adolf Schoepe would lead this newcomer, originally known as Gate-Way Manufacturing while in Los Angeles, in the hardware business to become the nation's largest producer of residential locks and Anaheim's largest employer by the 1960s. In 1957, Schoepe would sell his interest in the business in order to open another innovative hardware firm in Anaheim, Fluidmaster, Inc., which would revolutionize the toilet fill valve industry. Kwikset, today a division of Black and Decker, has left Anaheim, and the vacant factory site will house new residential development.

Fire gutted Anaheim's Mutual Citrus Products pectin plant on Monday morning, August 2, 1948. MCP was started in Anaheim in the late 1920s and became well-known to the housewife for their pectin product, which was used extensively in making jellies. The fire that started around 11:30 a.m. caused over $75,000 worth of damage to the plant, which employed about 150 local residents. In fighting the fire that raged for almost seven hours, the firemen used a 1915 Seagrave Pumper that performed better than a newer fire truck the fire department used. (Photograph by James F. Cowee; courtesy of Jim Cowee.)

Frank Belmont arrived from his native Italy in 1907 and eventually made his way to Anaheim where, in 1942, he built the modern Granada Packing House on Atchison Street. By 1944, it was the nation's largest independent (non-Sunkist) orange packer, shipping 80,000 boxes of local fruit. A public-spirited man, Belmont was a significant contributor to the local Community Chest drive and was a regular speaker on local citrus affairs. It was a significant local tragedy when on January 7, 1950, Granada Packing burned to the ground. By this time, excess packing capacity was available locally, and Belmont relocated his operation to nearby Fullerton. Belmont's citrus brands of Santa Anita, Granada, and Belmonte faded into memory when the plant closed in 1960.

# Two

# 1950–1959
## "Welcome to the Happiest Place on Earth"

Disneyland had just celebrated its first anniversary when this photograph was taken on July 25, 1956. Looking north, the new Santa Ana Freeway is seen crossing diagonally at the top of the scene. The new Harbor Boulevard–Santa Ana Freeway cloverleaf is also noted on the right as is Walt Disney's personally owned ride, the Disneyland Railroad, circling the park. Just left of center is the circus tent that housed "Professor" George J. Keller and his ferocious felines, and just to the right of the tent is the short-lived Junior Autopia. Anaheim officials gerrymandered a 768-acre annexation that enclosed the park and most of the surrounding land, located well out of town, on December 30, 1954.

The McNeil Construction Company's bulldozers are ready to grade the 160 acres north of Cerritos Street for Walt Disney's new concept amusement park, Disneyland. This dusty field, now devoid of the oranges and walnuts its previous owners nurtured, would, in just 11 months, open with a nationally televised event and would give American families a new vacation destination—Anaheim.

With opening day just a little more than a month away, this June 4, 1955, view looking south on Harbor Boulevard from the new Santa Ana Freeway (Interstate 5) overpass shows Disneyland's construction on the right. The earthen berm, right, was used by Disney "Imagineers" to shroud the park's visitors from the outside realities of Southern California and to support Walt's favorite ride—his narrow-gauge steam railroad. Just seven weeks after its public opening on July 18, 1955, Disneyland would welcome its one-millionth visitor.

The County of Orange Road Department took these historic views of Katella Avenue in 1955, looking east from West Street towards Harbor Boulevard. Just out of sight on the right was Katella Elementary School, which served the ranchers in this area. In just 10 more years, this block would see the construction of the Anaheim Convention Center, a number of hotels and motels, and eventually Disney's second theme park, Disney's California Adventure, in 2001.

This county photograph shows Katella Avenue in 1955 looking east from Euclid Avenue. The general rural atmosphere is broken by a small development of new homes on the left. "Quick Decline," a blight that was killing hundreds of acres of citrus per month, and the higher value of land for residential development gave the local citrus rancher every reason to burn groves off for new home construction.

By June 7, 1958, new motels were being constructed at the corner of Harbor Boulevard and Katella Avenue, lower right. Note Jack Wrather's new Disneyland Hotel at left center. Much of the Mauerhan Ranch was still under cultivation, however, in the lower portion of the Disneyland parking lot. Disneyland, only two years old, was already a major tourist attraction, having welcomed its 10-millionth guest by the end of 1957. The growth of the local motels and hotels would coincide with the increasing number of families who would visit what Walt Disney called the "Happiest Place on Earth."

In 1950, Anaheim's population had reached more than 14,000, and the fire department had just taken delivery of a new Seagrave "City Service Truck" that included a 65-foot aerial ladder. When parked in the old city firehouse behind Anaheim's 1923 city hall, the new truck stuck out over the Claudina Street sidewalk. Soon after, fire chief Rudy Nyboe arranged for a new headquarters fire station at 115 East Broadway. This early-1951 photograph shows all of Anaheim's firefighting equipment displayed in front of the new Broadway Street station. Chief Nyboe is seen at far right.

Anaheim's proud police force had this portrait taken in 1954 in front of the old station behind city hall at 110 South Claudina Street. The city's population was approaching 30,000, and the small police office, designed for a community of about 5,000, was now woefully overcrowded. Police chief Mark Stephenson quipped that the Anaheim jail was "the worst this side of Tijuana."

Beginning in 1924, Anaheim's Halloween celebrations have continued to grow every year to become a significant county-wide event. Highlighted by a nighttime parade that wound its way from La Palma Park to the downtown area, the event would begin with the Halloween Breakfast at City Park (now Pearson Park). The Anaheim revelers would be awakened at 6:00 a.m. by the Eltiste Calliope and looked forward to the hot coffee waiting for them. This October 1951 view gives a glimpse of the many attendees, most of whom dressed in costume for the occasion. The Halloween Parade continues today, more than 70 years after its inaugural march.

All Anaheim locals would participate in the Halloween festivities. The men in town would compete in a "Wiskerino" contest and if found clean-shaven, risk "arrest" and a trial in a kangaroo court. The ladies would also try their hand at costumes. Pictured are, from left to right, Alma Nickey, Patricia Loly, and Eleanor Faessel wearing Anaheim High School football uniforms.

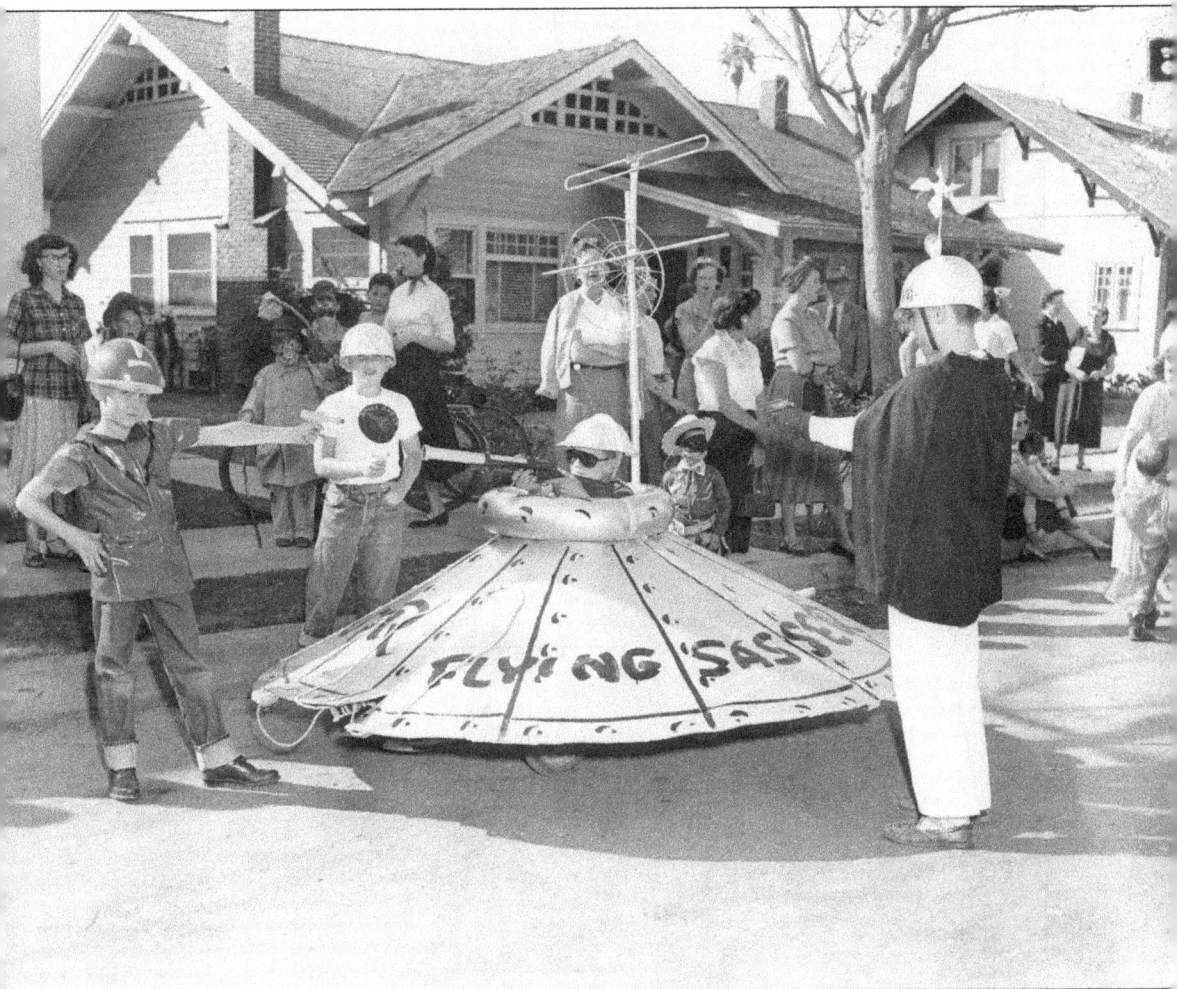

Most of the elementary schools would allow the children to march in the Halloween Kiddie Parade, an event well remembered by those old-timers who were able to participate. In the 1950s, space travel was a popular subject and these children entered their own homemade flying "sasser" in the parade. A young Lone Ranger is seen standing nearby. In addition to this event designed specifically for the town's youngsters, they also had an opportunity to paint Halloween scenes on the windows of Center Street businesses.

This c. 1950 view is looking south at the intersection of Lincoln and Manchester Avenues. Manchester was built in the 1930s and became the main road from Los Angeles into Orange County. Beginning in 1939, the state started planning the Manchester Freeway, but the onset of World War II delayed its construction. Once what became known as the Santa Ana Freeway (Interstate 5) arrived, it paralleled Manchester through most of Anaheim. In this photograph, Lincoln Avenue crosses at the lower portion of the photograph, and Manchester is seen sweeping across the left side. The Anaheim Cooperative Orange Association is visible near the Southern Pacific tracks at the center of the image.

Center Street (now Lincoln Avenue) looks east in this June 1951 view. The 1916 Hotel Valencia is pictured at the southeast corner of Lemon and Center Streets with Anaheim's favorite department store, the 1925 SQR (Schumacher, Quarton, and Renner), at the southwest corner adjacent to the S. W. Kress Building. In this era before regional shopping centers, downtown Anaheim was a viable business district.

This c. 1951 aerial view of Anaheim looks northeast with the intersection of South Los Angeles Street (now Anaheim Boulevard) and Santa Ana Street in the upper center of the photograph. Anaheim's landmark 1907 water tower on Los Angeles Street can be seen at upper right. The six-story Kraemer Building is seen at the top center. Fewer orange groves are seen as early residential development was beginning to take hold. The orange grove at left center, owned by the Pressel family, still exists today as the last reminder of Anaheim's citriculture past.

This composite photograph shows the interior views of an orange packinghouse and a meatpacking plant and a small inset of oranges. These images are examples of Anaheim's business enterprises at mid-century. Soon the dependence upon the cultivation of citrus would end, however, and modern research and electronic and defense firms would dominate the community's economy.

Alex Morales Sr. began selling his wife's homemade tamales in Anaheim in 1906 from a horse-drawn wagon. The Alex Tamale Company opened this factory in the 1920s at 415 South Olive Street. The family-run company was finally incorporated as Alex Foods in 1951 and continues today as part of Don Miguel Mexican Foods.

Northrop Aircraft opened its Anaheim Division in early 1952. Located on a 33-acre site at 500 East Orangethorpe Avenue, the 250,000-square-foot building housed manufacturing and office facilities. Nortronics, as it was later known, employed several thousand workers and was the first of several defense and electronic firms that would call Anaheim home.

Anaheim's mayor, Charles A. Pearson, was joined at the ground-breaking of the new Pacific Coast Borax laboratory on September 19, 1956, by the firm's vice president, George A. Connell; Dr. Howard Steinberg, manager of Organic Research; Harry Gower, manager of Land Department; and James McWaters of Security First National Bank. Located at 412 Crescent Way, the firm that would soon become known as U.S. Borax would employ 100 professionals, technicians, and support staff at their new Anaheim facility.

The Autonetics Division of North American Aviation opened in Anaheim in 1957. Later purchased by Rockwell International and then Boeing North American, it became Anaheim's largest aerospace employer, at one time employing over 30,000. Covering a large campus-like area along East La Palma Avenue, this facility would produce defense and space systems integral to the nation's security and Anaheim's economy.

Downtown Anaheim was still a local shopper's delight, with stores that catered to all interests and pocketbooks. In addition to the landmark SQR store, a J. C. Penney, S. H. Kress, and other locally owned businesses were popular with the residents. A major shift in shopping patterns would soon occur when the largest retail center outside of Los Angeles would open just a short distance west of Anaheim's historic downtown. Center Street shopping would now begin a downward spiral from which it would never recover.

On September 29, 1954, Mayor Pearson, along with Ed Carter, president of the Broadway-Hale Department store chain, and local chamber of commerce leaders, broke ground for the new $12 million Anaheim Center. Conveniently located at the Santa Ana Freeway–Euclid Street off-ramp, this new regional shopping center opened in October 1955 with the Broadway as the county's largest department store. Almost immediately, Anaheim's downtown businesses began to feel the effect of this new local shopping opportunity; the center began to attract business from all parts of the county.

The popularity of the Anaheim Center would lead the Robinsons Department Store chain to open a new store in 1962 anchoring the north end of the center. Modern in every respect, the new Robinsons and the seven-year-old Broadway, as well as the new smaller stores that adjoined them, eventually sounded the death knell for Anaheim's old downtown. Eventually Anaheim Center's Broadway and Robinsons stores also succumbed to redevelopment in 1993–1994. Sculptor G. Tsutakawa's tower fountain originally installed in 1963 still exists today, however, as one of Anaheim's "Art in Public Places" significant pieces.

By 1958, Anaheim's population had risen to more than 70,000 and covered almost 22 square miles. Still with only one library facility, the venerable 1908 Carnegie-donated building at Broadway and South Los Angeles Streets (now Anaheim Boulevard), meeting the literacy needs of the expanding community were difficult. Anaheim addressed this by purchasing a bookmobile in 1958 that would take library materials directly to the residents in the city's outlying areas. This program continues to serve Anaheim's diverse population, offering both printed and electronic media to the residents.

Anaheim's founding in 1857 brought about a large community celebration recognizing its centennial on September 8–13, 1957. The major event of the Anaheim Centennial was the Centurama, held at the La Palma Park stadium. This outdoor pageant, which included hundreds of Anaheim residents playing various historic parts, played to sold-out crowds for its run. Almost every church, school, fraternal, business, ladies, and civic group were represented in marches, songs, parades, and skits. Here Western Floatcraft is hanging banners advertising Anaheim's 100th birthday party.

As part of the city's centennial, the Anaheim Public Utility Department was recognized by *Western City Magazine* and the Mueller Company in August 1957. The caption of this magazine photograph reads, "These seven men represent 216 years of service to the Anaheim Public Utilities Department. From left to right: Mr. Oren H. Morey, 32 years; Max B. Moody, 26 years; A. J. "Tony" Hund, 31 years: Vernon C. Wright, 33 years: August F. "Gus" Lenain, 22 years; George F. Oelkers, 34 years; and Vard Hannum, 38 years."

Anaheim's centennial involved all types of promotions. A truck emblazoned as a paddy wagon would patrol the city streets and pick up hapless residents as a good-natured stunt to further advertise Anaheim's 100th birthday.

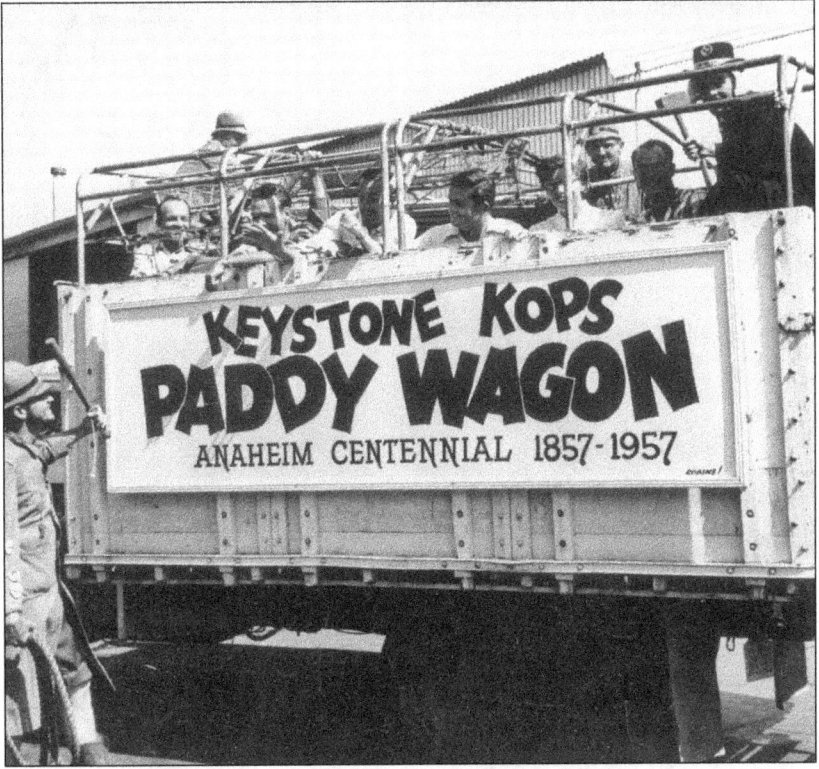

KEYSTONE KOPS
PADDY WAGON
ANAHEIM CENTENNIAL 1857-1957

KANGAROO KOURT
GUILTY AS CHARGED

Dutch Boy Paints

Good-naturedly, Mayor Pearson is placed in stocks (provided courtesy of Carle and Son's Wood Products) to serve his "sentence." The final and perhaps most significant centennial highlight was the assembly of a time capsule buried at the Anaheim Mother Colony House on West Street and marked to be opened in September 2007 by the community's schoolchildren. When opened as part of Anaheim's sesquicentennial, it will connect the children of 2007 to the civic hoopla of a much-smaller 1957 Anaheim.

By 1959, Anaheim's population was approaching 100,000 and covered almost 25 square miles. The city council, realizing the city needed to make major capital improvements, created five citizen-based subcommittees to study different areas of concern. Parks and recreation, library services, police and fire, city hall, and public utilities were all carefully studied in order to determine what improvements were required to bring Anaheim into the 1980s. The Public Utility Subcommittee is pictured here inspecting one of Anaheim's electrical facilities. From left to right are George Oelkers, utility director; Vard Hannum, retired utility superintendent; M. W. Martenet Jr., past city councilman; Bruce Cook, pipeline contractor; Myrtle Wilson; and Gus Lenain, water superintendent. This group recommended that almost $13 million be spent for utility improvements over the next 16 years. Similar recommendations were voiced by other subcommittees.

40

# *Three*

# 1960–1969
## "America's Hub of Happiness"

*Anaheim, California*

By the 1960s, Disneyland was already an international travel destination, and to serve this tourist industry, hotels, motels, restaurants, and other tourist-centered firms sprouted on the major streets surrounding the park. The landmark Disneyland entrance sign from Harbor Boulevard is seen at left center. The Matterhorn attraction and the expanded monorail system can be seen in the background of this early-1960s postcard view.

A new style of architecture, coined "Googie" by writer Douglas Haskell, found its best expression in the area around Disneyland. This eclectic abstract style, which used many components of modern technology, often was used in a manner that made the buildings appear to "hang from the sky." Al Stovall's Space Age Motel across from Disneyland included a number of space-age themes that were a common component of the Googie-style design.

Anaheim's Wonder Bowl incorporates several Googie themes, from the floating ball sign to the forward and future look of its entrance. Other Anaheim landmarks considered to follow the Googie style are the Anaheim Stadium "Big-A" scoreboard and the Anaheim Convention Center's flying saucer–shaped arena.

Although more modest, and located away from the Disneyland resort, the Sandman Motel located on East Lincoln Avenue also incorporates common Googie themes in its free-form monument sign and the neon sandman.

The SANDMAN MOTEL
1248 E. Center St.
Anaheim, Calif.

The La Palma Chicken Pie Shop at 928 North Euclid has invited in locals and tourists alike for the last 50 years with this Googie-featured sign. The neon blinking chicken, combined with the angular forms of the sign, all hearken to the Googie style. The restaurant's interior is a time warp to the 1950s with hanging white sphere lights, pink and aqua blue walls, and a chocolate-brown ceiling. This Anaheim landmark is still popular with the residents today, some who may not appreciate the building's architecture but who do love the chicken.

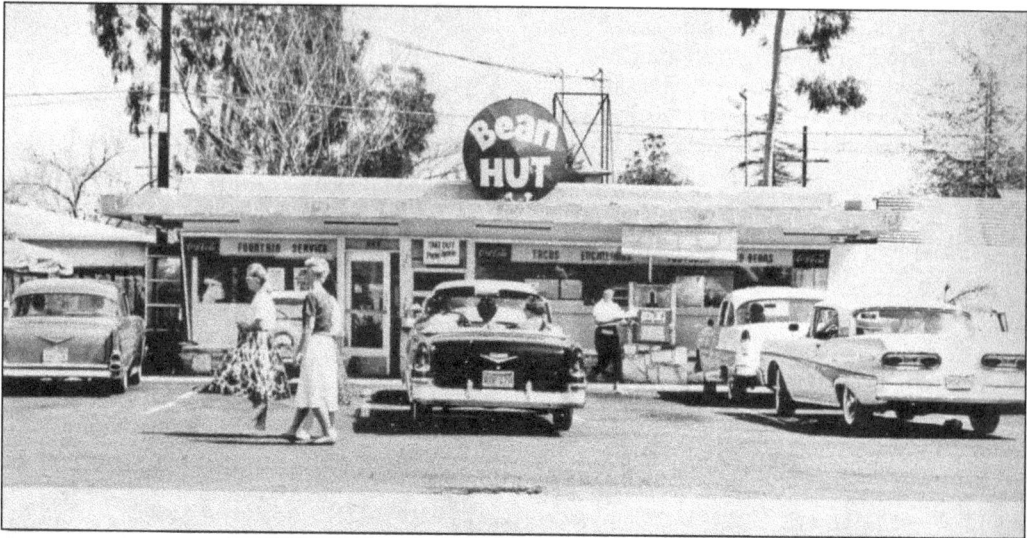

Ask any local high school kid in Anaheim during the 1950s and 1960s where the place to "hang out" and "be seen" was and a unanimous answer would be the Bean Hut. Properly named the La Palma Drive-In, this landmark fast-food restaurant at 940 North Los Angeles Street (now Anaheim Boulevard), once known as the Flying Saucer, featured real homemade Mexican food by Joe Cano (who also designed Anaheim Halloween parade floats for years). Its easygoing atmosphere, modestly priced good food, and carhop service attracted the locals in their Fords, Chevys, Dodges, and Plymouths, often to the dismay of their parents.

Martenet Hardware, known as the place in town that had just about everything tucked away in boxes accessed by rolling wooden ladders, celebrated their 50th year in business in 1960. Started in 1910 by his father, M. W. Martenet, Morris Jr. ran the store after his father's passing in 1959. Morrie, as he was known, served the Anaheim community as a city councilman from 1930 to 1942 and was still considered a good political analyst even in his later years. Pictured in this 1960 photograph taken on the store's anniversary are, from left to right, Arlowine "Tootie" Martenet (keeping a close eye on her husband), Marie Lenain, and Morris W. Martenet Jr. Although sold by the family in 1979, the business continues today at 1640 East Lincoln Avenue.

On April 27, 1962, the city unveiled a 38-foot pylon marking the name change of City Park to honor Anaheim's longtime mayor, Charles A. Pearson. While the name change was made official by city council action almost two years earlier, the planning, funding, construction, and an emergency repair due to an arson attempt on the fiberglass over the steel pylon delayed the ceremony. Pearson, at the microphone, is flanked by city council members and his beloved wife, Sarah (third from right).

Anaheim's police force was growing to meet the safety needs of the "fastest growing city in America," as Anaheim was known at the start of the 1960s. Police chief Mark Stephenson's force now boasted 20 motorcycles compared to the single bike the department owned in 1955. In 1963, the new Harbor Boulevard Police Station was dedicated, allowing the force to finally move from its cramped office on Claudina Street. This 1961 photograph was taken in the parking lot of Disneyland with Anaheim's police force fanned out for the camera.

This 1962 view is looking east on Center Street (now Lincoln Avenue). Anaheim's favorite department store, the SQR, is on the right with the Hotel Valencia across Lemon Street. Constructed in 1916 by John Ziegler as one of the area's best hostelries, the Hotel Valencia, by this time, was showing its age and was now catering to weekly rate customers. The Fox Theater still attracted many of the downtown locals, but the area had unfortunately already passed its prime.

Arriving in downtown Anaheim from the south in 1962, this would have been the scene as one was about to cross Broadway. The Pickwick Hotel offers weekly rates on its rooms, and its first-floor commercial tenants pay modest rents. Many downtown buildings are now owned by absentee landlords with little stake in the community. By the late 1970s, after several studies and decades of debate, Anaheim leaders would declare its historic downtown and some adjoining residential neighborhoods beyond repair, and a redevelopment program called Redevelopment Project Alpha would attempt to revitalize Anaheim's core.

In 1960, Anaheim's $33 million Capital Improvement Program included almost $13 million for utility infrastructure improvements. Anaheim's voters again supported the expansion and upgrades of its municipally owned water and electric utility. The city's growth required new water transmission mains and a new 60-million-gallon reservoir to meet the expected doubling of its population by the 1980s. The first delivery of 36-inch-diameter pipe receives an inspection by city officials in front of city hall in this 1961 scene.

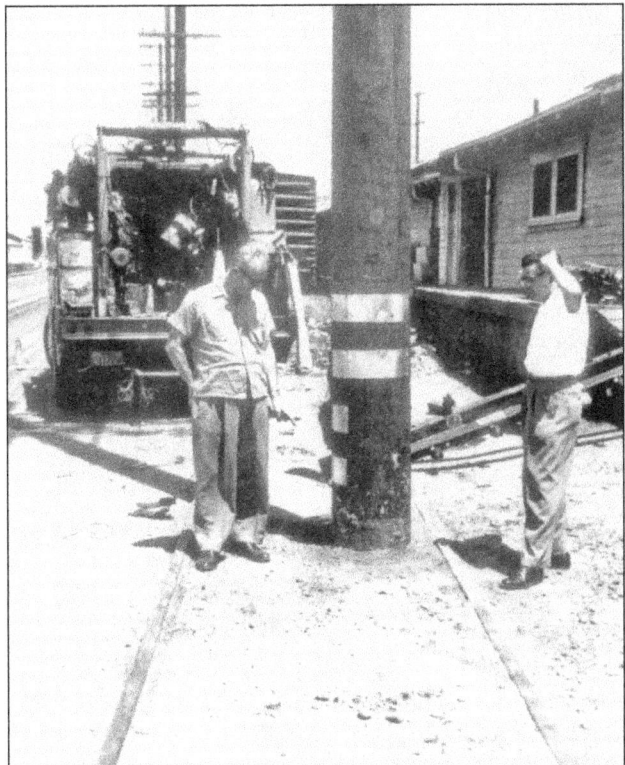

As Anaheim's area increased, so did the need to expand its citizen-owned electric utility into the newly annexed neighborhoods. A massive utility expansion followed in the 1960s to upgrade Anaheim's water and electric systems. This required the placement of a new power pole between the rails of an abandoned railroad spur at Santa Ana Street and South Los Angeles Street (now Anaheim Boulevard). Here Max Moody, superintendent (left), and Del Boisseranc, assistant superintendent, ponder the situation in this December 1961 scene.

Fire Station No. 2 was built for protection of the newly annexed area on Anaheim's western boundary. While actually not in the city, this facility included training facilities for the firefighters. The group portrait here shows both Anaheim's volunteer and paid firemen assigned to this station. Pictured from left to right are (first row) Robert Brunot, Robert De Groff, James Heying, Dick Pebley, Elred Lamb, James Hund, N. Nelson, and Frank "Frenchy" LaSaout; (second row) Thomas Lawler, Robert Lawler, Chet Kuebler, Bill Pebley, G. "Whitey" Earp, Jim Epperly, Harley Hesse, Herbert Davis, and fire chief Edward Stringer.

Anaheim's old fire headquarters station at 118 East Broadway was inadequate to serve a population that had grown to 133,000 by 1963. As part of the city's $33 million Capital Improvement Program in the early 1960s, this new two-story headquarters building was built at 500 East Broadway.

By the dawn of the 1960s, Anaheim's historic 1908 Carnegie Library building at 241 South Los Angeles Street (now Anaheim Boulevard) was unable to meet the needs of a population exceeding 104,000. As part of the city's Capital Improvement Program, a new two-story, $1.1 million building at 500 West Broadway was built on the site of the old Rimpau orange grove. Dedicated on February 23, 1964, this 67,500-square-foot facility continues as the city's Central Library and Administrative Office. As Anaheim's 150th birthday approaches, five branches and two bookmobiles have joined the Central Library to serve the community's literacy needs.

Anaheim's growth west through aggressive annexations more than doubled the city's size between 1955 and 1960. Seen here in 1962, city leaders broke ground for Anaheim's first branch library at 2650 West Broadway. Named in honor of Elva L. Haskett, Anaheim's first children's librarian, this branch served Anaheim's west side until replaced by a new, greatly enlarged branch dedicated on May 20, 2006.

After Pastor John C. Quatannens organized the St. Boniface Parish to build a much-needed larger church building, the long-remembered old 1903 church at 500 West Center Street (now Lincoln Avenue) was razed in March 1964. Here the students of the St. Boniface Elementary School watch as the old church's 87-foot steeple begins to fall under the attack of the demolition contractor's crane.

Anaheim's fourth St. Boniface Catholic Church edifice was dedicated in 1962. Located in the 500 block of West Center Street (now Lincoln Avenue), this modern structure replaced the parish's 1903 building located at Harbor Boulevard and Lincoln Avenue.

On May 2, 1964, entertainer Jack Benny again visited the cadets of St. Catherine's Military School. Benny, one of Hollywood's most famous comedians, was invited to participate in the school's Diamond Jubilee, and he is seen here relating his show business experiences to the attentive crowd of cadets and guests who attended the celebration. Jack's first visit to the school was on Monday April 24, 1947, when "Mr. Sunday Night" himself came into town to attend the Civic Progress Week's banquet held at the Elk's Club.

Anaheim's sphere of influence crossed the Santa Ana River into the Olive Hills when the city, through a land swap with the City of Orange, located a site for its new high-elevation reservoir. When dedicated on August 7, 1962, this 60-million-gallon facility was one of the largest of its type in the county. This 1966 scene shows the sparsely populated hilltops still surrounding the lake at this time.

In March 1966, Paul Van Doren opened a 400-square-foot retail store at 704 East Broadway and began selling a new line of sneakers that he and his partners produced in their small factory behind the store. From this inauspicious beginning, the Van Doren Rubber Company went on to become famous as the manufacturer of Vans, a line of shoes that were all the rage with Southern California skateboarders and young BMX cyclists.

Dixie Cup built a large modern plant in Anaheim in 1952 at 901 East South Street. It was one of Anaheim's early employers and anchored a new industrial area south of downtown.

Commercial development kept pace with Anaheim's residential growth in the 1950s and 1960s. Menasha Container Corporation of California located their new paperboard box manufacturing facility at 601 East Ball Road in 1955 in order to capture part of the Los Angeles market share. This facility was sold to the Weyerhaeuser Corporation in 1981 and continues today at the same location.

Anaheim was home to a number of electronic firms by the early 1960s. Ling-Altec, Inc. Communication Systems established an Anaheim facility at 1515 South Manchester Avenue in 1957, just a short walk from Disneyland.

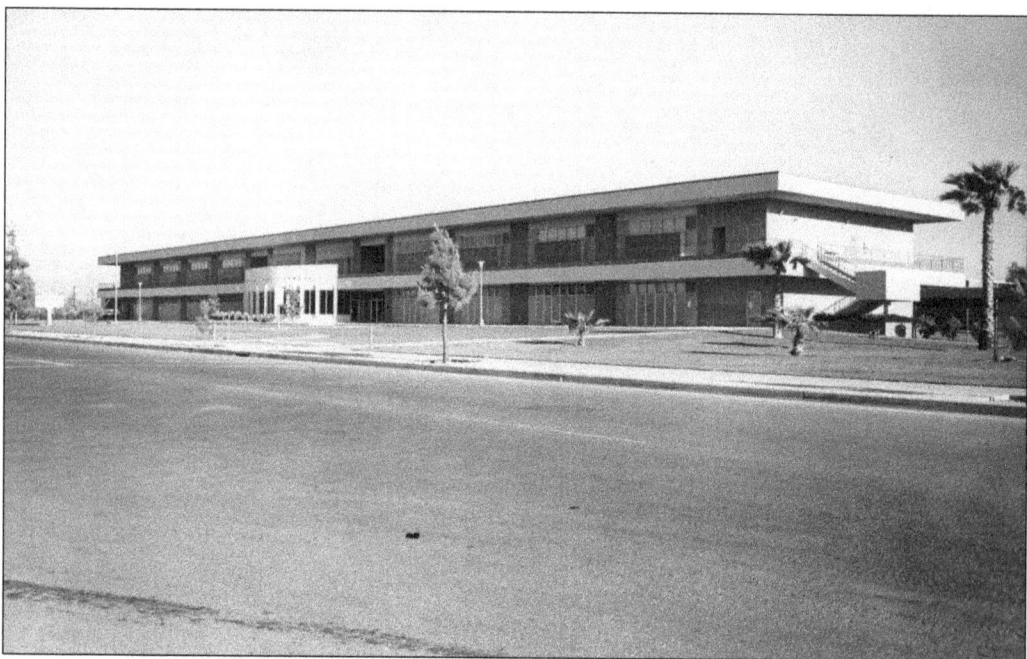

As Anaheim's residential population grew, so did the need to expand schools to meet the educational needs of the growing number of children in the community. Katella High School at 2200 East Wagner Avenue was dedicated in 1966 and immediately began serving the expanding neighborhoods on the city's eastern border.

Theatric producers Sammy Lewis and Danny Dare opened Melodyland Theater on July 3, 1963, with Betty Hutton and Harve Presnell appearing in *Annie Get Your Gun*. This unique 3,270-seat theater-in-the-round was a fine complement to Disneyland's entertainment just a short walk away. Although initially popular with both local and out-of-town patrons and offering a number of top names in entertainment, the theater continued to suffer financially. After a number of owners and a long stint as a Christian center, this facility was razed to make room for increased hotel and tourist facilities in the Disneyland resort area.

Disneyland continued to add new attractions just as its creator, Walt Disney, predicted. This 1967 aerial view looking to the northeast shows the construction of what became two of Disneyland's favorite attractions—the Haunted Mansion and the Pirates of the Caribbean. By this time, the monorail track crossed West Street to connect to the Disneyland Hotel, the first crossing of a public street by monorail in the country. In the distance can still be seen a few of the area's rapidly diminishing orange groves.

In September 1963, Anaheim mayor Rector "Rex" Coons contacted the Los Angeles Angels about the possibility of the team moving to Anaheim; team owner Gene Autry was looking to relocate out of Los Angeles and was already negotiating with Long Beach. Once talks broke down because of Long Beach's insistence that the name of the city be incorporated into the team's name, Anaheim offered to provide a stadium for the team with no such name restriction. This August 31, 1964, photograph shows the ground-breaking for the new 43,000-seat Anaheim Stadium with 4,000 excited fans looking on.

Cowboy star turned professional baseball team owner Gene Autry joins Anaheim mayor Odra "Chuck" Chandler (center) and Anaheim Stadium builder Del Webb (right) in wielding the shovels for what many will call the "biggest moment in Orange County sports history." Anaheim assumed the $16 million cost of the construction itself after the Orange County Board of Supervisors, thinking the project was too risky, backed out of the deal.

Once ground was broken, construction started immediately in order to make the April 9, 1966, opening game deadline. The Knutzen, Allec, Reynolds, Ross, Lenny, Bruggeman, and Wagner families would soon see their 144 acres of oranges and alfalfa be turned into what would become nicknamed simply the "Big-A."

A proud Gene Autry is seen in front of the still-unfinished 230-foot-tall "Big-A" scoreboard in this February 1966 view. From the time Autry purchased the Los Angeles Angels in 1960 for $1.4 million, the cowboy singer had been looking for a new home for his promising team. By 1963, Orange County's population had swelled to 1,024,810 residents, and Anaheim felt that the region's sports-starved residents could support a professional baseball team.

With less than two months to opening day, Anaheim's city manager, Keith Murdoch, surveys the Anaheim Stadium construction site. Murdoch, who came to Anaheim in 1950, was known for his "can do" attitude and team-building management style. By his retirement in 1976, Anaheim's population had increased 14-fold, and the city had become an international tourist destination and a center for sports and entertainment in Southern California.

This c. 1970 aerial view of Anaheim Stadium, looking northeast, still shows some of the few remaining orange groves in the area. On April 9, 1966, after dedication ceremonies officiated by Anaheim's mayor, Fred T. Krein, the Angels played their first exhibition game against the San Francisco Giants before a crowd of 40,735 fans, losing 9-3. The first regular-season game between the Angels and the Chicago White Sox was held on April 19.

In order to promote the city at both the "Big-A" and the new Anaheim Convention Center, an Anaheim city flag was designed by Bud Nagel, the city's public information officer in 1967. In this April 11, 1967, photograph, Anaheim mayor Fred Krein (far left) is presenting the new flag to Gene Autry (second from right) in a pregame ceremony. Bob Reynolds, president of Angels Baseball, (to the right of the mayor) and California state senator John McCarthy (to the left of Autry) join in the event.

The first football game held in Anaheim Stadium was an Angelus League high school matchup on November 3, 1966, between Santa Ana's unbeaten Mater Dei Monarchs and Anaheim's Servite Friars. Twenty thousand cheering fans saw the Monarchs run to a 36-6 victory. This was soon followed on December 9 by the most anticipated Anaheim High School football game since the days of Mickey Flynn in 1957. The unbeaten Anaheim Colonists were pitted in a CIF (California Interscholastic Federation) semifinal game with the still-unbeaten Mater Dei Monarchs. A crowd of 32,808 excited fans watched this battle of the two Orange County high school football powerhouses, a non-championship game attendance record. After a difficult first half and a second half that included an 83-yard Anaheim drive, coach Clare Van Hoorebeke's tired Colonists marched off the field with a 12-7 victory.

The first professional football game ever played at Anaheim Stadium took place on August 2, 1967, when the New Orleans Saints played the Los Angeles Rams in an exhibition game. The Rams took the lead in the first quarter and later won the game with a 16-7 score. Approximately 13 years later, the Rams would take up permanent residence at the "Big-A."

Disneyland continued to attract visitors from around the world but remained usually only a summertime destination. In order to build more year-round business, Anaheim's civic leaders proposed the construction of a convention center. A concept that had been discussed in local circles since the 1930s, the Anaheim Convention Center finally became a reality when it opened in July 1967. The May 9, 1965, ground-breaking for the new $14.5 million facility was held in typical Anaheim fashion, pushing the plunger to set off a charge of dynamite in a dusty field off Katella Avenue.

This May 5, 1966, construction view of the new Anaheim Convention Center shows its location tucked into the corner of orange groves south of Katella Avenue. The facility's flying saucer–shaped arena was still under construction but would be ready for the summer grand opening in 1967.

Once opened, the 400,000-square-foot Anaheim Convention Center began to attract groups from all parts of the country who found the facilities, local climate, and the location across from Disneyland attractive. After a number of major expansions and several cosmetic renovations, the Anaheim Convention Center is now the largest of its type on the West Coast and anchors one of Southern California's most-visited tourist areas.

The close relationship between Mickey and his friends, seen here arm in arm, and the Anaheim Convention Center is evident in this spring 1967 photograph. The partnership with Disney; the convention center; the many hotels, motels, and additional tourist-driven services; and the city's national sports franchise have moved the economy of Anaheim and Orange County far from the agriculture of their birth.

In 1969, the newly elected president, Richard Nixon, an Orange County native, was welcomed at the Anaheim Convention Center upon his return home from Washington, D.C. Anaheim has welcomed Hollywood stars, recording artists, and heads of state to the convention center since its opening in 1967.

During the 1960s and 1970s, the Convention Center Arena was the place for concerts. In addition to such acts as the Beach Boys, Johnny Cash, John Denver, Peter Frampton, Elton John, and Willie Nelson, the King himself, Elvis Presley, played to a sold-out crowd in 1973. Fans lined up for three days in advance to ensure they got a ticket.

Anaheim's Lincoln Avenue was brightly decorated for the 1970 Christmas season. The old downtown merchants were still doing all they could to keep their customers, although a few of the old firms had already closed. Anaheim's elected leaders were already planning a significant change for the historic center of the city; a move they hoped would breathe new life into the slowly deteriorating area.

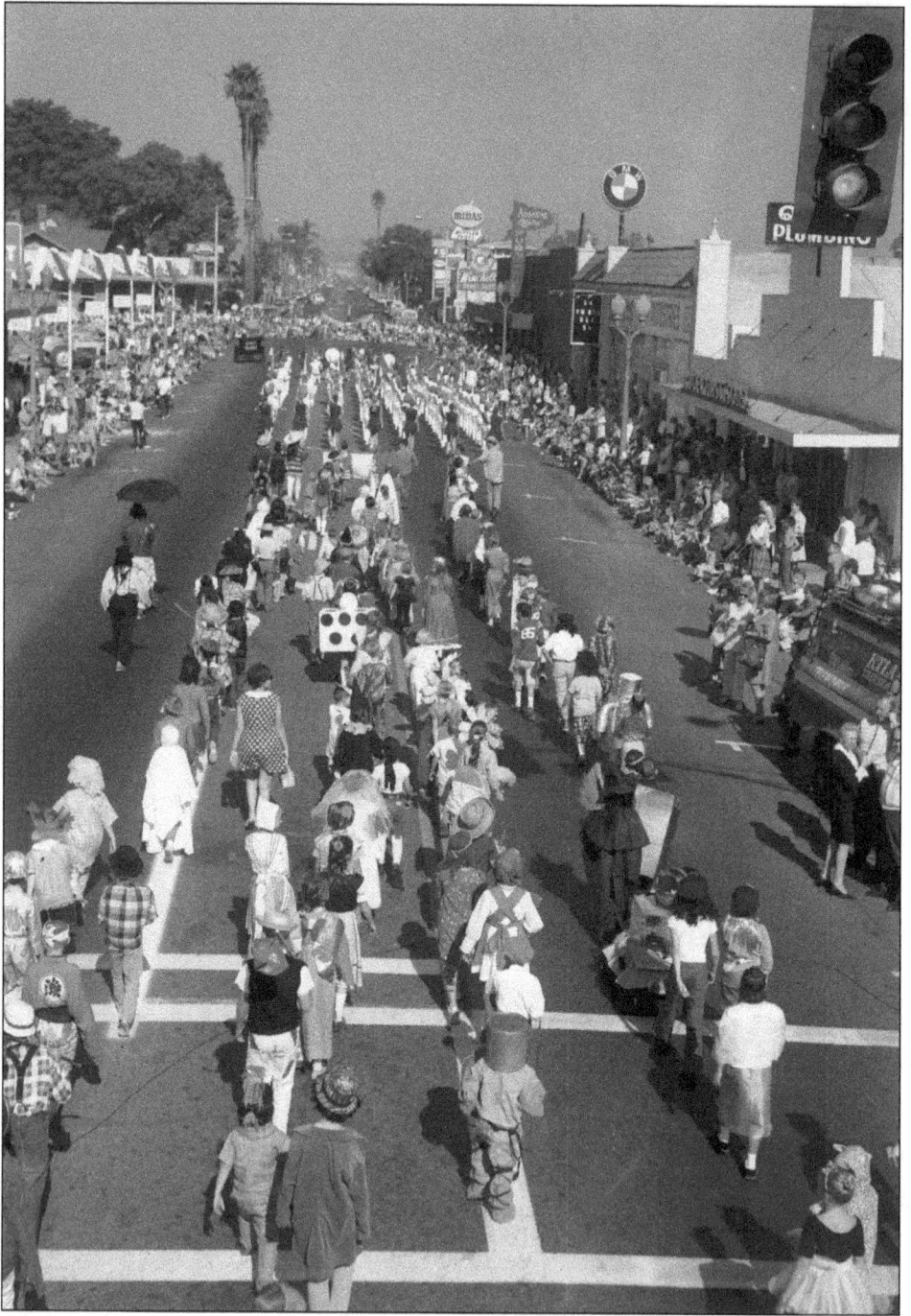

Anaheim's Kiddie Parade has been a part of the annual Halloween celebration for many decades. A chance for the school-age children to leave classes early was always an additional incentive to ask the parents to prepare a costume. The locally televised 1969 parade is pictured marching north on Los Angeles Street (now Anaheim Boulevard) from Cypress Street. In less than a decade, this street scene will have changed completely with the arrival of Anaheim's downtown redevelopment, and many of these longtime businesses will be only memories.

# Four

# 1970–1979
## "Dreams Come True in Anaheim"

Anaheim's city government would manage through another decade of unprecedented growth and begin a process of downtown revitalization, the effects of which are still being felt today. The department heads had a group portrait taken outside the Anaheim Convention Center on the morning of January 14, 1970. Pictured are, from left to right, (first row) Robert M. Davis, assistant city manager; David B. Michel, chief of police; Thornton E. Piersall, public works director; Dene M. Williams, city clerk; Keith A. Murdoch, city manager; Joseph B. Geisler, city attorney; and Douglas K. Ogden, finance director; (second row) Alan S. Orsborn, development services director; Gordon W. Hoyt, utilities director; Roy E. Heissner, personnel director; Edward J. Stringer, fire chief; Thomas R. Liegler, stadium and convention center director; John J. Collier, parks and recreation director; and William J. Griffith, library director.

Anaheim's residential march east towards the Santa Ana River was well underway by the late 1960s. Neighborhoods east of State College Avenue were being carved out of the old orange groves to support the new residents, many working for one of Anaheim's defense firms such as Autonetics or Nortronics. This view of the intersection of East Lincoln Avenue and St. College Avenue around 1970 shows the new homes to the east and northeast. Anaheim had now become a city of 166,000 persons and covered 33 square miles.

Anaheim's landmark 1925 six-story Kraemer Building is visible in the center of this 1972 view. Anaheim's city hall, built in 1923, is across Lincoln Avenue. Built for a community of 6,000, it was now serving the municipal government needs of a city of nearly 200,000 and had been deemed unsafe by two engineering studies. In 1970, an election was held in which Anaheim voters expressed the desire that a new civic center, when the city was ready to build one, should be located in the area occupied by the city hall.

66

To serve the needs for meeting space, classes, and exhibits in Anaheim's expanding west side, the city debuted their new Brookhurst Community Center on April 8, 1978. The $1.1 million project was substantially funded through a $750,000 federal public works grant. Although originally planned for the Modjeska Park area, following neighborhood concerns of traffic and parking issues, a location adjacent to Brookhurst Park was selected at 2271 West Crescent Avenue.

The City of Anaheim had entered floats in the Pasadena Rose Parade 17 times by the time this entry rolled down Colorado Boulevard in 1971. Including 23 of Walt Disney's most famous characters and decorated with more than 100 varieties of flowers, this entry named "Dreams Come True in Anaheim" won the tournament's Theme Prize.

Less than 10 years after its opening, the Anaheim Convention Center was expanded by an additional 135,000 square feet to accommodate increased use of the facility. This June 21, 1973, view shows the construction of the additional exhibit hall space known as Betterment I.

The January 1974 completion of the convention center's $16.9 million Betterment I expansion is pictured here. The 9,000-seat, Googie-style arena sits just off Katella Avenue. The new, large Royal Inn Hotel is seen at the lower left corner as are additional motels across from the convention center on Katella Avenue.

On January 7, 1971, Anaheim mayor Jack Dutton, center, accepted the new California Angels pennant from club owner Gene Autry, right. At left is Angel's club president Robert Reynolds. Dutton, an Anaheim native, was instrumental in getting Autry to consider Anaheim as the new home for his professional baseball club.

Anaheim leveraged its new civic asset for concerts and stage shows once the success of an August 1968 USO show featuring Bob Hope attracted a crowd of more than 30,000. In the fall of 1969, a Billy Graham Crusade drew more than 350,000 people to the stadium over a 10-day period. In this 1970 view, the Assembly of the Men of Goodwill is staging their sold-out event at Anaheim's "Big-A."

To bolster the finances of the "Big-A," the city of Anaheim offered its unique outdoor venue for a variety of uses. The Who performed the first rock concert in the stadium on June 7, 1970, and drew 30,000 fans. The Osmond Brothers arrived for a September 8, 1972, performance and hammed it up for the camera before their concert opened.

Mayor Dutton is pictured here giving the Osmond Brothers troupe an Anaheim City Council Proclamation at their 1972 concert. The Osmonds played before 29,832 fans, with reportedly 95 percent of the audience consisting of mothers and daughters. Concession sales took a marked decrease when 15-year-old teen heartthrob Donny took the stage.

The American Freedom Train made a scheduled stop at Anaheim Stadium from January 9 to 13, 1976. Former Southern Pacific steam Locomotive No. 4449 and its 10-car exhibit train backed onto a little-used spur in the "Big-A's" parking lot and was an immediate sell-out, with lines reaching around the stadium. Designed to celebrate the country's bicentennial, the train featured significant historic items such as the Liberty Bell, copies of the Constitution and Declaration of Independence, and unique items such as Judy Garland's dress from *The Wizard of Oz*.

Anaheim Ebell Club president Jackie Terrell (left) hosted a 95th birthday party for the club's charter member, Miss E. Kate Rea, in March 1971. Rea taught for 20 years in Orange County, served on the Anaheim Library Board for 45 years, was an Anaheim School District trustee for 16 years, and organized Anaheim's first PTA in 1909. Her and her sister Ella's names were combined by their father, John Rea, to create "Katella," which the highway outside their south Anaheim ranch was named. The Ebell Club, Anaheim's oldest women's society, celebrates its centennial in 2007.

Beginning on June 17, 1972, Disneyland inaugurated its new summer event, the Main Street Electrical Parade. The parade, consisting of floats themed to Disney movies, was lighted by half a million tiny lights. This event quickly became one of Disneyland's most beloved traditions.

Four of Disneyland's icon rides are seen here, including the Skyway that opened on June 23, 1956, and the monorail, Matterhorn Bobsled, and Submarine Voyage rides that opened on June 14, 1959. In 1961, the Monorail was extended across West Street to the Disneyland Hotel. The Skyway ride closed in 1994, followed by the closing of the Submarine Voyage, the original "voyage through liquid space," in September 1998.

72

Anaheim city councilman John Seymour is pointing to the future location of a residential housing development and a future Anaheim Golf Course in this c. 1970 photograph. On October 30, 1970, 4,200 acres of Mr. and Mrs. Louis Nohl's grazing and avocado ranch were deeded to Santa Anita Consolidated with the intent of creating a new affluent planned community named Anaheim Hills. The City of Anaheim soon purchased 300 additional acres of the Nohl Ranch to build a tournament-class golf course and park sites.

Anaheim's population almost doubled in the 1960s, again straining the city's water supply. In 1963, the voters approved another $4.9 million water system construction bond that enabled a new 920,000-gallon reservoir to be built in the Nohl Ranch hills. When dedicated on April 5, 1970, the 50-acre lake, along with the adjacent Lenain Filtration Plant, gave Anaheim the highest water storage per capita in Southern California. In just a few short years, residential development would surround this site.

By 1972, Anaheim's new public golf course opened to positive reviews. Built among the rolling hills but with fairways that are primarily level, the course offers both the novice and experienced player a great game.

By August 1971, a joint venture created by Texaco Ventures, Inc., and Anaheim Hills, Inc., purchased additional property in the hills above the Santa Ana River for residential development. The Anaheim Hills plan called for construction of some of the finest homes in Orange County as well as tennis clubs, a saddle club, riding and hiking trails, a variety of parks, shopping centers, and places of worship. This early-1970s photograph shows an example of the contoured grading required before home construction could begin.

In July 1972, Westridge, the first Anaheim Hills neighborhood, opened, selling all 325 homes by early 1975. Additional residential expansion in the Santa Ana Canyon continued when the Bauer, Oak Hills, and Wallace ranches were developed in the mid-1980s. Nearly 1,000 acres of land has been dedicated to public agencies to ensure the community maintains its rural atmosphere.

On July 19, 1973, the Anaheim City Council took action to create a redevelopment plan, Redevelopment Project Alpha, for the central city area. Despite significant public outcry from residents who wanted to save a few of the more historically significant downtown buildings and reuse them, complete demolition of the 200-acre area would result. This spring 1978 photograph shows the final sale at Anaheim's beloved, although now little shopped, SQR store. The peeling gold leaf on the once proud SQR sign indicates the general look and feel of the downtown area at the time.

By October 1978, the proud SQR department store, built in 1925 of reinforced concrete by the Schumacher, Quarton, and Renner families, was reduced to landfill.

The Cotler's for Men sign was now just rubble. A popular men's store located at 118 West Lincoln Avenue, Ken Cotler and his family's store are now just a memory.

Anaheim residents could no longer shop at Lind Rexall Pharmacy at 144 West Lincoln Avenue nor could they walk over to 132 West Lincoln and "Meet Joe Hurst and Wear Diamonds" any longer after the demolition crews started their work in the fall of 1978.

Virgil Isbell, the longtime owner of the Office Barber Shop at 129 East Lincoln Avenue, had already retired and sold the business to his friend and partner Paul Wimer by the time the bulldozers arrived. Virgil and Paul served most of the downtown businessmen as well as multiple generations of Anaheim families, many of whom had their first "big boy" haircut there.

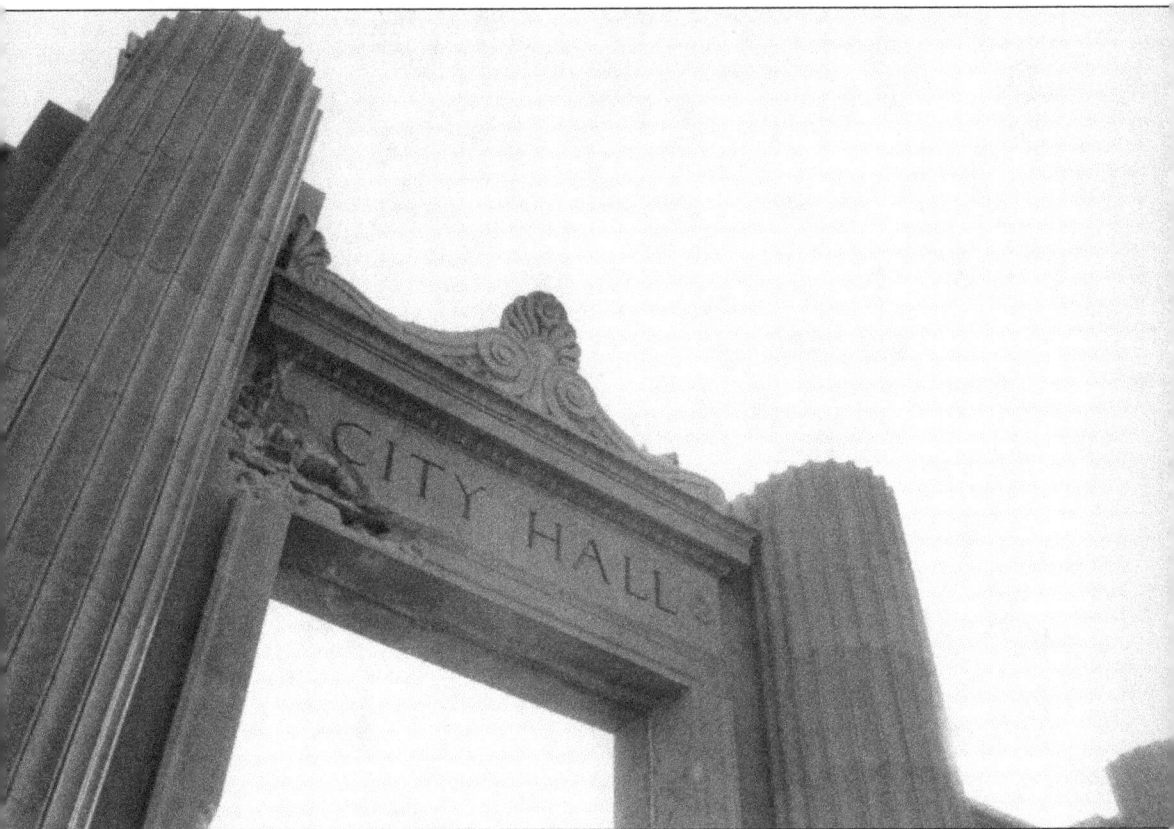

All that remains of Anaheim's once proud 1923 city hall is the entrance silhouetted against the afternoon sky. Located at 204 East Lincoln Avenue, it was the seat of government for what would become "the fastest growing city in America" during the 1950s and 1960s. It would be replaced by a much larger and more modern structure befitting a city of 221,000 residents, which was fast becoming the center for sports and tourism in Southern California.

After four citizen committee reports that reviewed the need for a new city hall, three space usage surveys regarding office utilization, two engineering reports about the deterioration of the old 1923 city hall, and a 1970 election where the community voted to have a future civic center built downtown, construction finally got underway for Anaheim's new Civic Center on March 1, 1978. Here Mayor Bill Thom, assisted by Miss Anaheim, strikes the first hammer blow to begin construction.

Anaheim's new seven-story, 133,285-square-foot Civic Center was the first structure built on the "Superblock," bounded by Lincoln Avenue, Anaheim Boulevard, Broadway, and Philadelphia Street. Upon completion, the city government could now house most of their offices in one location rather than in 16 buildings spread throughout the city.

This aerial view of the downtown area taken on January 31, 1979, shows the construction of Anaheim's fourth city hall structure. The 1923 city hall is still standing in the upper right of the photograph. By the end of the decade, only two of Anaheim's old downtown buildings will remain standing—the 1925 Kraemer "skyscraper" and the community's beloved 1908 Carnegie Library building.

Redevelopment Project Alpha comprised 200 acres roughly bordered by Harbor Boulevard to the west, Broadway to the south, East Street to the east, and Cypress Street to the north. An integral part of the plan was to realign Lincoln Avenue around the redeveloped area in order to give as much space as possible for future development. This late-1979 view looking east, with Harbor Boulevard at the lower part of the photograph, shows Lincoln's future route as well as the extent of the demolition up to this point.

Anaheim's new Civic Center was dedicated on June 24, 1980, and featured a 33,804-square-foot, two-story structure; a seven-story, 94,356-square-foot office tower, and a 5,125-square-foot city council chamber. This building would remain the dominant structure in the downtown area for several years because Redevelopment Project Alpha's construction timetable would drastically change as investment funds for development dried up in the 1980s.

# Five

# 1980–1989
## "DREAMS BECOME REALITIES"

In 1981, local artist Emigdio Vasquez and student artists Louie Hernandez, Silvia Mendoza, and Perry Ware produced this large mural to recognize 124 years of Anaheim progress. Hanging today in city hall, it memorializes the various personalities, landmarks, and scenes of early and contemporary Anaheim history. (Photograph by George Fenton; courtesy of the Anaheim Museum, Inc.)

Carroll Rosenbloom's Los Angeles Rams were seeking a new home away from the Los Angeles Coliseum in the late 1970s. Anaheim's "can do" spirit went into high gear, and at a July 25, 1978, press conference, it was announced that an agreement had been reached to bring the Rams to Anaheim. A $33 million stadium expansion soon followed, which would enclose the stadium in order to expand it to 70,500 seats for the opening of the 1980 football season.

Before the expansion that would enclose the field, the landmark "Big-A" scoreboard would have to be moved. The 23-story, 240-ton Big-A would need to travel 1,300 feet from its original location behind the center field wall to a spot adjacent to the 57 Freeway. The scoreboard that for 13 years had recorded the Angel's hits and misses would be hoisted onto giant rollers and, by July 17, 1979, arrive at its new location.

This early-1980 construction view of the enlarged Anaheim Stadium shows the field now completely enclosed and the "Big-A" scoreboard relocated next to the 57 Freeway. This $33 million project would increase the seating to over 70,000 and bring professional football to Orange County.

This view of a Rams and Packers game shows the attendance the Rams drew in their early years at the "Big-A." Commercial development has now erased all traces of the area's agricultural past, and Anaheim, once known for its Valencia oranges, would now be internationally recognized for its professional sports teams.

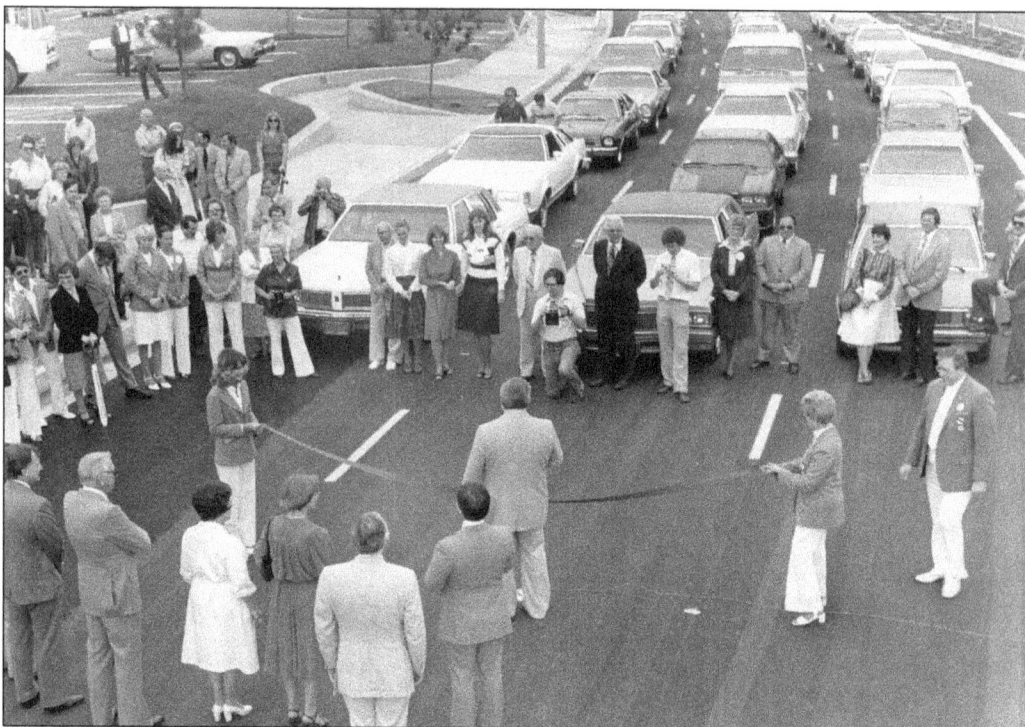

Part of Anaheim's downtown revitalization required the realignment of Lincoln Avenue one block to the north. On October 9, 1980, a ribbon was cut at the corner of Lemon Street to reopen the first section of Anaheim's main east-west thoroughfare. Additional work building an underpass for the Santa Fe Railway tracks further east would delay the total completion of the new Lincoln Avenue roadway until the end of 1988.

By the mid-1980s, only parts of the new downtown envisioned by Redevelopment Project Alpha were realized. The tightening of investment funds curtailed what Anaheim leaders felt would be a rapid rebuilding of Anaheim's downtown core. This view facing southeast shows the new Lincoln Avenue alignment with the six-story Kramer Building, now housing the El Camino Bank, in the background. By this time, most of the old businesses that had moved out of the area and were waiting for new development to welcome them back had closed permanently.

The first major new building in the Superblock area was Anaheim's imposing Civic Center building. A number of Anaheim's old downtown buildings are still standing, such as the vacant 1923 Angelina Hotel in the upper left corner of the photograph in this mid-1980s view. Ganahl Lumber had already moved to Ball Road by this time to make room for the new Lincoln Avenue east end realignment.

The new Anaheim Towne Center, including a Safeway Supermarket and a Sav-On Drug store, had arrived by the mid-1980s. Occupying space long held by Anaheim's original downtown businesses, they supplied the daily needs of the surrounding community. Anaheim's vacant 1926 Pickwick Hotel still holds out hope that it might be spared.

In an effort to save a few of Anaheim's more historically significant buildings, the Anaheim Historical Society was formed in 1976 to raise the community's awareness of the value of some of their buildings and neighborhoods. Although many meetings were held with Anaheim's leaders requesting the adaptive reuse of some of the old downtown buildings, few successes resulted. In May 1982, the Samuel Kraemer Building, built in 1924, was added to the National Register of Historic Places due to an application submitted by Diane Marsh and Andrew Deneau, society members. This act, in addition to loud public outcry about the loss of all of Anaheim's downtown history, helped preserve this building.

The marquee of the Garden Theater, Anaheim's downtown adult movie house, tells the story of the final fate of this building in this September 27, 1983, photograph. Although most demolition began in 1978, additional building demolition was carried out as late as 1988.

On March 21, 1984, Anaheim's nearly 100-year-old chamber of commerce moved to this new, modern, glass building at 100 South Anaheim Boulevard, adjacent to the new Civic Center structure. Looking north, the tall palm trees in the upper left are located at Pearson Park.

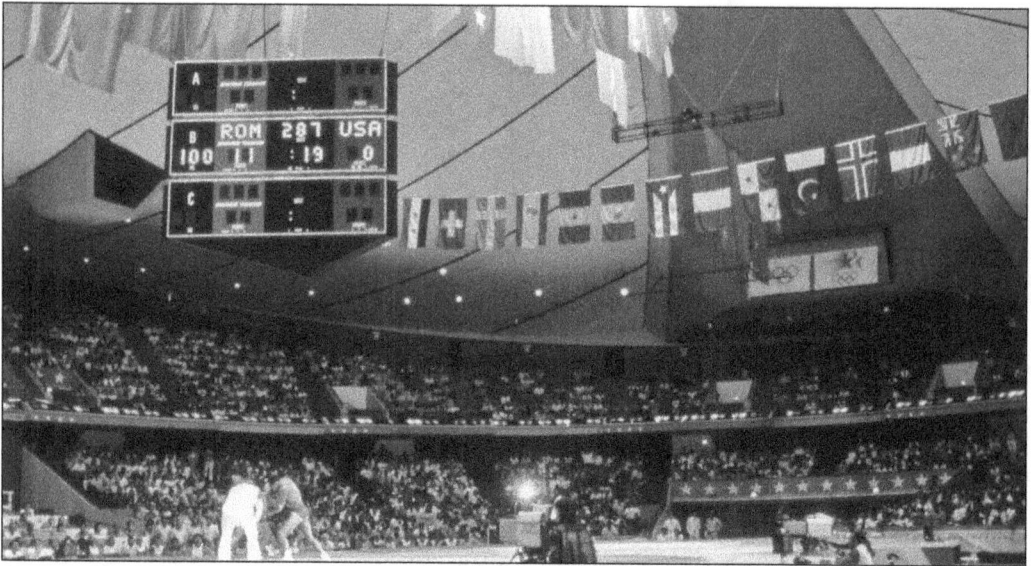

When the Summer Olympics visited Los Angeles from July 28 to August 12, 1984, the Anaheim Convention Center Arena was selected as one of several Orange County venues for specific events, such as Greco-Roman wrestling. Other venues chosen included Mission Viejo, which hosted the Olympic long-distance cycling road races; California State College, Fullerton that offered team handball; and Coto De Casa, which held the modern pentathlon.

To commemorate what would have been Walt Disney's 84th birthday and to recognize Disneyland's 30th year in operation, Anaheim sponsored a million-balloon salute called Skyfest. The December 5, 1985, event included representatives from Disneyland, Anaheim city government, schools, and local nonprofit organizations. One thousand tubes, each holding 1,000 balloons, were all launched at exactly 2:00 p.m. along Katella Avenue between Harbor Boulevard and West Street, literally blanketing the sky with the multicolored, helium-filled orbs. This launch far exceeded the previous world's record of a 384,800-balloon release in Japan the previous year.

Anaheim's convention center continued to grow throughout the 1980s with the addition of 150,000 square feet of exhibit space in 1982. The $17.8 million project was inaugurated with a ground-breaking accompanied by the Ringling Brothers Circus, which was playing at the Convention Center Arena at this time. Here Anaheim city officials are joined by a number of circus clowns as they prepare to break ground for Betterment II.

The Redevelopment Project Alpha area also included a number of Anaheim's oldest residential neighborhoods. A number of these historic homes were saved by the City Redevelopment Agency and relocated to a newly created street called Vintage Way, east of the Santa Fe Railway tracks. This street is now lined with several of Anaheim's most historic homes, painstakingly restored by their owners. This view is of the 1911 Joseph Bennerscheidt house being moved from its original site at 219 South Lemon Street to its new location during the early morning hours of November 14, 1984.

Anaheim's 1908 library building, funded with a $10,000 grant from steelmaker tycoon Andrew Carnegie, remains one of Anaheim's most beloved public buildings. Though it was originally earmarked for demolition, significant public pressure to save it resulted in the city finally agreeing to renovate the building and allow the fledgling Anaheim Museum, Inc., to occupy it for $1 per year. Mayor Bill Thom signed a City Council Resolution on February 28, 1978, that designated the property as a historical library, research center, and museum. After a $781,000 retrofit, a lease was finalized in October 1986, and the Anaheim Museum opened on November 14, 1987.

As an early fund-raiser, the Anaheim Museum created a coverlet highlighting a number of the area's finest historic buildings. Wednesday museum volunteer Eleanor Faessel is seen holding up an example for the camera with the museum pictured in the background.

In order to provide the necessary public safety requirements for the Anaheim Hills area, a new fire station was added in the early 1980s. Station No. 10 was located in temporary facilities while a permanent modern structure was built at 8270 East Monte Vista. In conjunction with its Water Services Division, Anaheim's fire department has earned the city a "Class 1" rating by the Insurance Services Office, representing exemplary public protection, one of only 10 communities in California to do so.

One of the early public buildings built in the Anaheim Hills area was the new Canyon Hills Library Branch. Mayor John Seymour presented the $1.4 million facility to the community on July 11, 1981. The 18,000-square-foot public library provided a lounge, a children's area, and a community room in addition to 90,000 books for the rapidly expanding region.

This 1987 view of the Home Savings and Loan Building at the corner of Harbor Boulevard and Lincoln Avenue shows the building's mural depicting significant people and events in Anaheim's history. Home Savings commissioned many of these murals for their buildings in the communities they served. The Anaheim mural, created by artist Millard Sheets, features George Hansen, the "Father of Anaheim," as well as Madame Helena Modjeska, a world famous tragedian that once called Anaheim home. Washington Mutual acquired Home Savings in 1988.

The Union Pacific finally reached Anaheim in May 1923, and although additional lines in Orange County were planned, Anaheim remained the terminus of this branch line. The attractive passenger station soon closed but remained a shipping point for the region's orange crop for many years. By the 1970s, it had been relegated to other uses, the most recent as a school supply store. This September 16, 1987, photograph shows the depot before its eventual move across Lincoln Avenue and reuse as a child care center, a victory for historic preservationists.

On September 9, 1987, the Anaheim Arts Council and the Community Services Department dedicated the new *Fountain of the Arts* in front of the Pearson Park Theater. The quatrefoil-shaped tiled pool, which replaced the 38-foot Charles A. Pearson monument, was the newest addition to the Art in Public Places Project sponsored by the Anaheim Arts Council.

Sixty-four years of hard use finally required the replacement of Pearson Park's original 1923 baseball diamond grandstand in August 1987. Originally designed by Anaheim's local architect, M. Eugene Durfee, and built at a cost of $10,665, it was a popular spot to watch both men and women's softball games on a warm summer evening.

By the fall of 1987, the old wooden Pearson Park grandstand was rebuilt using modern materials but in almost the exact style as the original 1923 structure. This action on the part of the Community Services Department was much appreciated by a community that had recently lost most of its historic downtown to redevelopment.

The Pickwick Hotel at 225 South Anaheim Boulevard was originally named the El Torre by the Pickwick Stage lines in 1926. Built at a cost of $110,000, it was one of Anaheim's better hotels for many years. By the 1970s, it had fallen on hard times and was earmarked for demolition as part of Redevelopment Project Alpha.

Despite a hard-fought campaign to save it, the Pickwick succumbed to the bulldozers on June 2, 1988. Thought too costly to upgrade to current seismic standards and in the way of future new development, the last of Anaheim's significant buildings would be reduced to pallets of used brick. Anaheim's eight-year-old Civic Center is seen across Anaheim Boulevard in this view.

# Six

# 1990–1999

## "WHERE THE WORLD COMES TO LIVE, WORK, AND PLAY"

When the year 1990 arrived, Anaheim had grown to a population of 279,408—an increase of over 50,000 in just 10 years. The agriculture that supported the early growth of the community had all but disappeared; only one small orange grove remained in the old downtown area. Development had moved the city limits both east and west, and the city now covered over 48 square miles. This view looking south shows the old downtown area at left center and Disneyland at the top of the photograph.

The idea of an indoor sports venue to complement Anaheim Stadium had been considered for several years. Discussions began in earnest in early 1989, and by July, Anaheim had agreed on an arena project with the Ogden Corporation. On July 25, 1990, plans for the new 19,500-seat state-of-the-art facility were accepted by the city council. The nearly $100 million project broke ground the following November and was finally named the Arrowhead Pond of Anaheim when a sponsorship agreement with Arrowhead Water was signed. Today the popular facility is branded as the Honda Center.

On March 1, 1993, the Anaheim Arena receives its first major tenant, the Mighty Ducks of Anaheim, a recently created National Hockey League expansion team owned by the Disney Corporation. Walt Disney chairman and CEO Michael Eisner (center) and his new team were welcomed to Anaheim by Mayor Tom Daly (right) and councilman Irv Pickler (left) on the still-unfinished arena floor.

The Anaheim City Council finally cut the ribbon on the steps of the arena on June 17, 1993, opening the newest sports venue in Southern California. Pictured with the ribbon are, from left to right, Frank Feldhaus, Fred Hunter, Mayor Tom Daly, Irv Pickler, and Bob Simpson.

Goaltender Guy Hebert, No. 31, was the first player chosen by the Mighty Ducks in the 1993 Expansion Draft, arriving from the St. Louis Blues. He claimed 60 of the first 84 wins in Mighty Ducks history. The Anaheim Arena was known as the Arrowhead Pond of Anaheim by this time through an exclusive sponsorship arrangement. Gwen Thums won the Duck's "Name the Mascot" contest with her entry, Wildwing.

The Walt Disney Company partnered with the city to build an ice rink downtown at the corner of South Clementine Street and Center Street Promenade. When opened in September 1995, this controversial Frank Gerry–designed building became a practice location for the Disney Mighty Ducks national hockey team. After Disney sold their interest in the Ducks, the facility was renamed Anaheim Ice.

With millions of tourists visiting Anaheim's attractions each year, the issue of efficient transportation between the various venues was always of concern. Beginning in early 1990, the city requested a study on the possibility of building a monorail system to connect Anaheim Stadium with Orange County's John Wayne Airport. This architectural rendering shows what the system might have looked like outside of the "Big-A."

On January 17, 1994, at 4:30 a.m., California suffered one of its most damaging earthquakes, registering a magnitude of 6.7 and having the highest ground acceleration ever recorded. Named the Northridge Earthquake for its epicenter, the quake caused significant damage to the Anaheim Stadium scoreboard more than 50 miles away. Weighing 17 tons, the scoreboard, installed when the stadium was enclosed in 1980, cost $10 million to repair.

When the Rams debuted at Anaheim Stadium on September 7, 1980, it was without the individual who was instrumental in bringing them to Anaheim, owner Carroll Rosenbloom, who had drowned the prior spring. After a 14-season 61-57 record, the Rams left Anaheim for St. Louis in October 1995.

When the Rams left Southern California in late 1995, the City of Anaheim announced that they would refurbish their 29-year-old stadium. At about the same time, the Walt Disney Company purchased a 25-percent stake in the Angels from Gene Autry, and after much negotiation in April 1996, Anaheim and Disney reached an agreement for the $100 million renovation and operation of the "Big-A." Disney completed the purchase of the Angels in 1998 after the death of the team's beloved owner, Gene Autry.

The Walt Disney Company contracted with Edison International for the naming rights of the stadium they had through the contract with the stadium's owner, the City of Anaheim. The construction that started in October 1996 reverted the structure back into a baseball-only facility, and removing the outfield seats restored the field to its original 1966 appearance. The stadium debuted in March 1998, just in time for the Anaheim Angels' opening day on April 1. Pictured are, from left to right, council members Tom Tait, Shirley McCracken, and Mayor Tom Daly, Nanette Sanchez (Miss Anaheim), and council members Lou Lopez and Bob Zemel.

Known for 30 years simply as Anaheim Stadium and fondly nicknamed the "Big-A," the controversial new name of Edison International Field of Anaheim was announced on September 15, 1997. Improvements to the facility included terraced bullpens in the outfield, widened concourses, new concession areas, state-of-the-art club-level suites, and landscaped courtyards. In addition to new family-oriented seating sections, three full-service restaurants were added, all of which restored the stadium's reputation as one of the country's best sports venues.

Anaheim's downtown redevelopment plan was delayed in the 1980s due to the lack of investment funds, leaving most of the 200-acre Redevelopment Project Alpha still vacant. In July 1990, the city finally broke ground for the $200 million Koll Anaheim Center. This project would include a new Pacific Telephone building, a new 11-story city hall annex building, parking structures and shops centered on the intersection of South Lemon, and a new street, Center Street Promenade, directly across from the new Civic Center. Anaheim Public Utilities participated in the funding of the city hall annex and became the main tenant of what became known as City Hall West.

By the early 1990s, several major projects had begun to fill in the redevelopment area. This view, looking southwest, shows the seven-story City Hall East Building at 200 South Anaheim Boulevard and the City Hall West Building across the street. The new chamber of commerce building is to the right. The parking lots seen directly in front are at the approximate location where Anaheim's 1923 city hall once stood. In 1996, ground was broken on this site for a much anticipated new community center.

By 1998, commercial development had filled in much of the 200 acres that were cleared for Redevelopment Project Alpha two decades earlier. Significant vacant areas still awaited final development, which was less than a decade away. A gradual change in city leadership, coupled with the increased awareness of the value of its historic neighborhoods, led the city council to designate much of Anaheim's original 1,165 acres as the Anaheim Colony Historic District in October 1997. Many of Anaheim's original neighborhoods would now see restoration through the property tax abatement incentive offered by the Mills Act.

The Anaheim Ballet was proclaimed the resident ballet company of Anaheim in August 1997. During the warm summer months, these talented performers are often seen at Orange County's oldest cultural arts venue, the 1927 Pearson Park Theater.

Ogden Entertainment opened Tinseltown, a faux Hollywood awards dinner show adjacent to Anaheim Stadium in November 1998. Renamed the Sun Theater in August 1999, it began to book first-rate talent and boosted the local concert scene. A 2001 opening of the House of Blues nearby drew talent and patrons away, however, forcing another new name and concept in December 2001. By September 2002, the City of Anaheim had purchased the Grove Theater and partnered with Nederlander Corporation to finally successfully manage the entertainment venue.

The rapid, little-planned development around Disneyland required a face-lift by the early 1990s. After a new sign ordinance was enacted, the kitschy collection of Googie-inspired signs along Harbor Boulevard would give way to a much cleaner, simpler street scene. Coupled with Anaheim's aggressive utility undergrounding program and the establishment of a special 1,100-acre Anaheim resort tax assessment district, the area centered around Disneyland and the convention center would become much more visitor friendly.

The Anaheim Convention Center continued to grow through the 1990s, adding 308,000 square feet through expansions in 1990 and 1993. The 15-story Hilton Hotel seen at the center of the photograph now featured over 1,500 rooms, making it one of the largest hostelries on the West Coast. The large Disneyland parking lot across Katella Avenue from the Anaheim Convention Center would soon see the transformation into a new theme park, adding to the popularity of Anaheim as a tourist and convention destination.

In May 1991, Disney announced plans to open WESCOT, a new attraction patterned after the company's EPCOT attraction located in Florida. A recession in the early 1990s, coupled with the Gulf War, depressed tourism, making the concept no longer economically sound. On July 17, 1996, Disney again announced the development of a new theme park to be called Disney's California Adventure, which would highlight the California lifestyle. Disneyland's parking lot would soon be transformed into a $1.4 billion attraction that would include a major hotel, dining, and entertainment venues.

By the late 1990s, Harbor Boulevard had taken on a much cleaner look due to major streetscape improvements that included improved landscaping and lighting and a new signage requirement. By now, the Anaheim visitor had a choice of over 20,000 hotel and motel rooms at which to stay and literally hundreds of places to eat. Anaheim was trying very hard to live up to its motto: "Where the world comes to live, work, and play."

Local artist Richard Turner created this beautiful Veterans Memorial located adjacent to the Anaheim Museum on South Anaheim Boulevard. Dedicated on December 4, 1999, this bronze and stone structure includes a circular water feature and recognizes the sacrifices made by the veterans through all of this country's conflicts.

# Seven

# 2000–2007
## "Always Fresh and Never Grows Old"

A three-phase $169 million expansion of the Anaheim Convention Center began in 1997 and was finally completed on January 8, 2000. This project expanded the facility's size by 40 percent, making it 1.6 million square feet. The main lobby would soar 190 feet, and the glass rotunda would welcome millions of convention attendees to Anaheim. In 2006, the Anaheim/Orange County area would see 44.9 million visitors who contributed a record $8 billion to the local economy.

Caltrans began improvements to Interstate 5, the main north-south thoroughfare through Orange County, in January 1997. The $1.1 billion project included widening the freeway from 6 to 12 lanes, new overpasses, and high occupancy vehicle lanes. Part of the improvements also included direct off-ramps to Disneyland's hotels and parking structures. The four-year project, completed in 2001, literally cut Anaheim in half, causing many local traffic problems. This view is looking north from Ball Road.

Disneyland's parking lot took on a new look in 2000 as the new $1.4 billion Disney's California Adventure was under construction. Guests would now park in the 10,000-car Mickey and Friends parking structure, the second largest such structure in the world, seen at the upper left. The new arts and crafts–style Grand Californian Hotel is taking shape at left center of this scene.

By 2001, the $4.2 billion public-private package, which included expansion of the Anaheim Convention Center, the building of Disney's California Adventure park, freeway improvements, new landscaping, signage, and utility improvements, was completed. Anaheim had created a special tax assessment district in 1996 for the 1,100-acre Anaheim Resort, which would continue to fund the local improvements and maintenance without burdening the taxpayers.

On February 8, 2001, Disney's California Adventure park would open amid controversy. Designed to re-create different California landmarks and be more adult-oriented than Disneyland, initial criticism was raised that the park was "not Disney enough." On May 5, 2004, the new Twilight Zone: Tower of Terror ride opened and immediately raised the new park's attendance. Disney management continues to refine the California Adventure concept, and the park's popularity continues to rise.

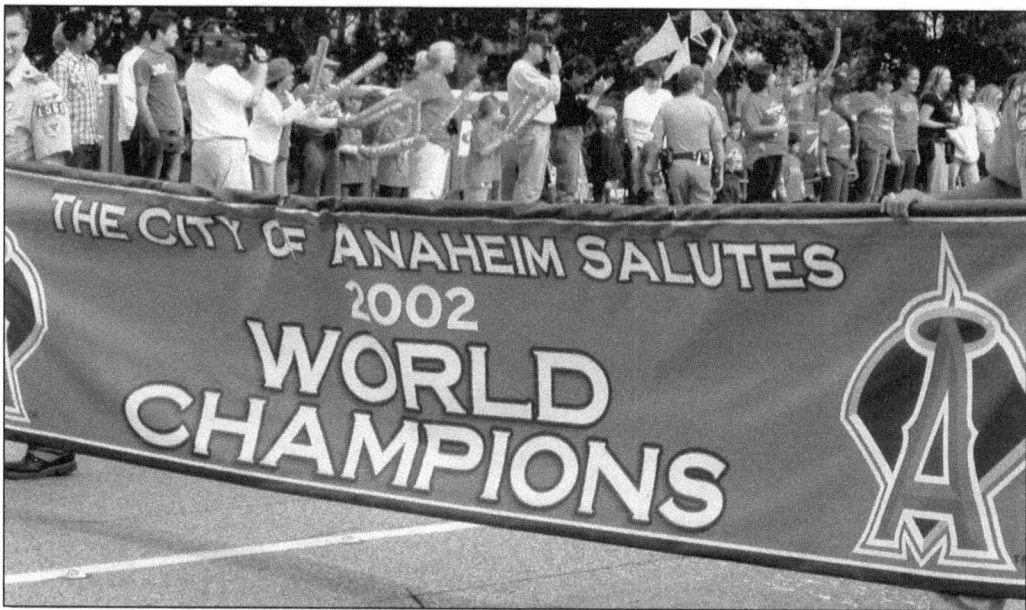

Although fans had always remained hopeful, what few thought possible actually happened in Game 7 of the 2002 World Series—the Anaheim Angels beat the San Francisco Giants 4-1 and came off the field as World Series champions. After 41 years of frustration and a near miss in 1995, the often-beleaguered Anaheim Angels brought home the trophy to their owners, the Walt Disney Company, on Sunday, October 27, 2002. When the long sought after World Series trophy was presented, the team's original owner's widow, Jackie Autry, was nearby holding Gene's old cowboy hat. In recognition of the trophy arriving in Anaheim, the city sponsored a celebration parade down Katella Avenue.

Finishing the 2002 season with a 99-63 record, the Angels were given a wild-card entry into the play-offs. After defeating the New York Yankees and the Minnesota Twins, the Angels claimed the American League pennant. The World Series would pit Anaheim against San Francisco in a seesaw battle that tied the teams at three games each. The pandemonium and the sound of the ThunderStix could be heard blocks away and showed the international television audience that Orange County had finally graduated into the national sports consciousness.

116

On May 15, 2003, outdoor advertising magnate Arturo "Arte" Moreno purchased the Angels from the Walt Disney Company, becoming the first Hispanic to own a major sports team in the United States. Utility deregulation problems that dogged Edison International led them to exercise their option to exit the 1998 naming rights agreement, and on December 19, 2003, the Angels announced that the stadium would be renamed Angel Stadium of Anaheim. The stadium, which had been nicknamed the "Big Ed" while the regional electrical utility held naming rights, was once again the "Big-A," much to the delight of the fans who had been told five years earlier to "Kiss it Goodbye" in a short-lived rebranding advertising campaign.

Arte Moreno soon changed the name of his team to the Los Angeles Angels of Anaheim, much to the dismay of the Anaheim City Council who felt an earlier contract with Disney would have kept the city's name more prominent. A yearlong lawsuit in which the details of earlier contracts between the city and the Disney Company were carefully examined resulted. The controversial verdict in February 2006 allowed Arte to keep Los Angeles in the team's name as long as it continued to include "Anaheim."

Following the creation of the Anaheim Colony Historic District in October 1997, owners of some of Anaheim's historic homes began the painstaking process of restoring them to their as-built original appearance. Such restored properties are eligible to receive property tax relief based on the 1972 Mills Act program, designed to encourage preservation of historic properties. The Colony Historic District includes over two square miles of Anaheim's original town site and includes about 1,100 structures of historic distinction. The historic two-story Mission Craftsman house located at 902 West Broadway is a clear example of the care that homeowners take to meticulously restore the exterior of their homes.

The Anaheim Colony Historic District received their new $1 million neighborhood park on March 16, 2002. Named George Washington Park in recognition of the George Washington School that once occupied the site, the new playground was a much-needed addition to this neighborhood. In 1878, the first bond issue of its type provided $10,000 to build Anaheim's Central School at this location. In 1932, the replacement school was named for George Washington on the bicentennial of his birth and occupied this site until 1980.

On February 10, 2006, former president Bill Clinton and California first lady Maria Shriver helped cut the ribbon on the Tiger Woods Learning Center. This 35,000-square-foot facility is the realization of a long-held dream of the golf prodigy who wanted to "provide students with a place to explore their dreams and open doors to new opportunities and potential career paths." Located on a 14-acre campus, this state-of-the-art student enrichment facility, which includes a unique solar electric curtain wall, sits adjacent to "Dad" Miller Golf Course. Woods attended Western High School and often played golf at "Dad" Miller.

By 2005, Anaheim's population had passed 342,000, and the literacy needs of its diverse population had exceeded the capacity of its solitary bookmobile. Designed to take the library directly to low-income, high-density neighborhoods, this program was inaugurated in 1958. Funded through a variety of methods, including state and federal grants, private fund-raising, and partnership with Anaheim's Public Utilities, this natural gas–powered second bookmobile arrived in September 2005.

The ribbon is cut to open the newly rebuilt Haskett Branch Library on May 20, 2006. After being closed for two years, the new facility, three times the size of the original, offers more than 70,000 books, magazines, and a wide selection of Spanish-language materials. The expansion of the facility was long championed by the West Anaheim Neighborhood Development group, which saw the need to rebuild the original 1962 facility to better serve Anaheim's expanding west side. Pictured are, from left to right, Mayor Pro-Tem Richard Chavez, Mayor Curt Pringle, council member Bob Hernandez, council member Harry Sidhu, and county supervisor Lou Correa.

The last remaining parcels of Redevelopment Project Alpha were finally contracted for construction in 2005. The CIM Group's $100 million project will fill the last seven vacant acres in downtown with mid-rise buildings containing about 400 housing units and over 50,000 square feet of retail space. In addition to the CIM Group, John Laing Homes has added 56 new houses to the downtown area on the site of the old Anaheim Truck and Transfer facility. This CIM architect's view is looking northwest across Broadway Street at the new Carnegie Plaza and Doria Lofts development.

As part of the CIM Group's mixed-use residential project, 13,000 square feet of new space will incorporate the city library's Local History Room and a state-of-the-art exhibit facility. With the historic Carnegie Museum building just across a new plaza, the combined facilities will operate together as a new organization, named the Muzeo, adding a new force to the cultural arts of downtown Anaheim. Unprecedented public involvement in the planning process guaranteed that these new structures will mirror the architectural styles of Anaheim's 1920s and 1930s streetscape.

On October 17, 2006, Anaheim unveiled the new two-acre Roosevelt Park in the Anaheim Hills area. This new park is within walking distance of several neighborhoods and provides additional green space and recreational opportunities. Unique to this park, however, is that it sits on top of a much-needed new electrical facility required for the continued expansion of the hill neighborhoods of Anaheim.

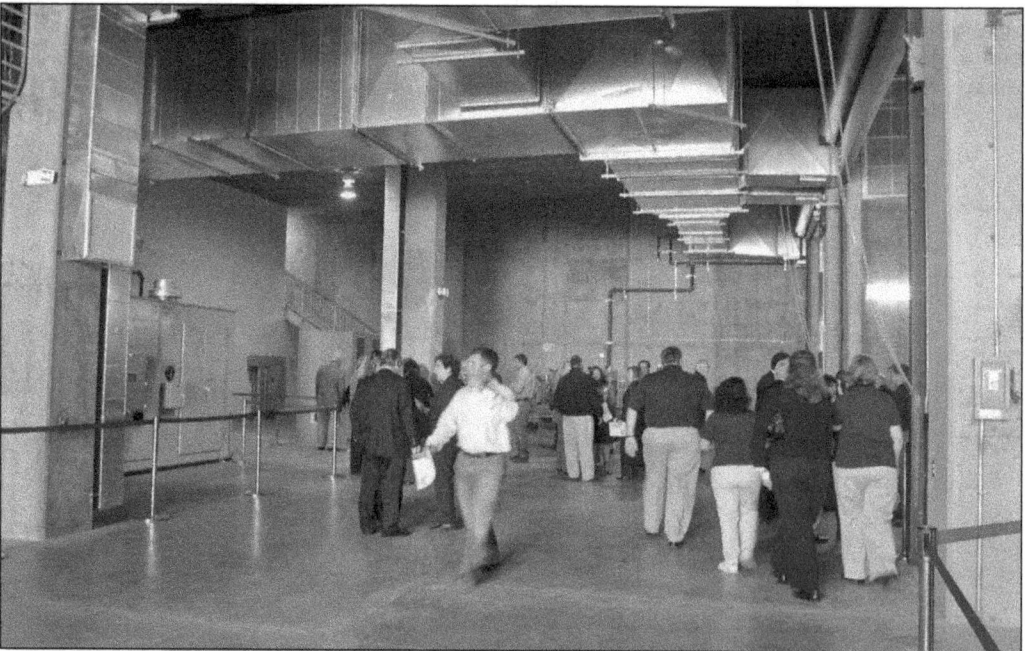

In an important partnership that provided the neighborhood with a much-needed park, Anaheim's citizen-owned public utility built the first underground electrical substation in the country. The $19.5 million project serves the electrical utility needs of the local area as well as the Irvine Company's future 2,500-home Mountain Park development at the eastern edge of the city.

124

A modern 13,500-square-foot gymnasium was built adjacent to the city's police substation in the Anaheim Hills area in late 2006. Dedicated on January 20, 2007, this sports facility will meet the needs of the many youth basketball leagues that cannot find sufficient court space. This $4 million gym will be the latest addition to the complex, which already includes a police substation, a community center, and a new branch library. (Courtesy Elon Schoenholz.)

On September 12, 1857, surveyor George Hansen purchased 1,165 acres of land for what would become Anaheim. As Orange County's oldest incorporated city, Anaheim will celebrate its sesquicentennial in the year 2007, and 15 months of events befitting such a birthday are planned. In addition to the kick-off concert held on October 5, 2006, and a new Tournament of Roses float in January 2007, an Anaheim-Orange County Walk of Stars along Harbor Boulevard, a photograph contest, historic building dedications, a 1957 Anaheim Centennial Time Capsule unearthing, special stamp cancellations, and a gala New Year's Eve send-off will all add to the celebration.

Carl Karcher and his late wife, Margaret, the founders of the Carl's Jr. restaurant chain and longtime Anaheim residents, received their star, just a short walk from Walt Disney's star on Harbor Boulevard, as part of the Anaheim–Orange County Walk of Stars program on January 16, 2007, Carl's 90th birthday. They were honored for their entrepreneurial and philanthropic contributions throughout Anaheim and Orange County. Pictured here are, from left to right, (first row) Carl Leo Karcher, son, and Carl D. LeVecke, grandson; (second row) CKE CEO Andy Puzder, founder Carl Karcher, Anaheim mayor Curt Pringle, and Walk of Stars president Bob Alexander.

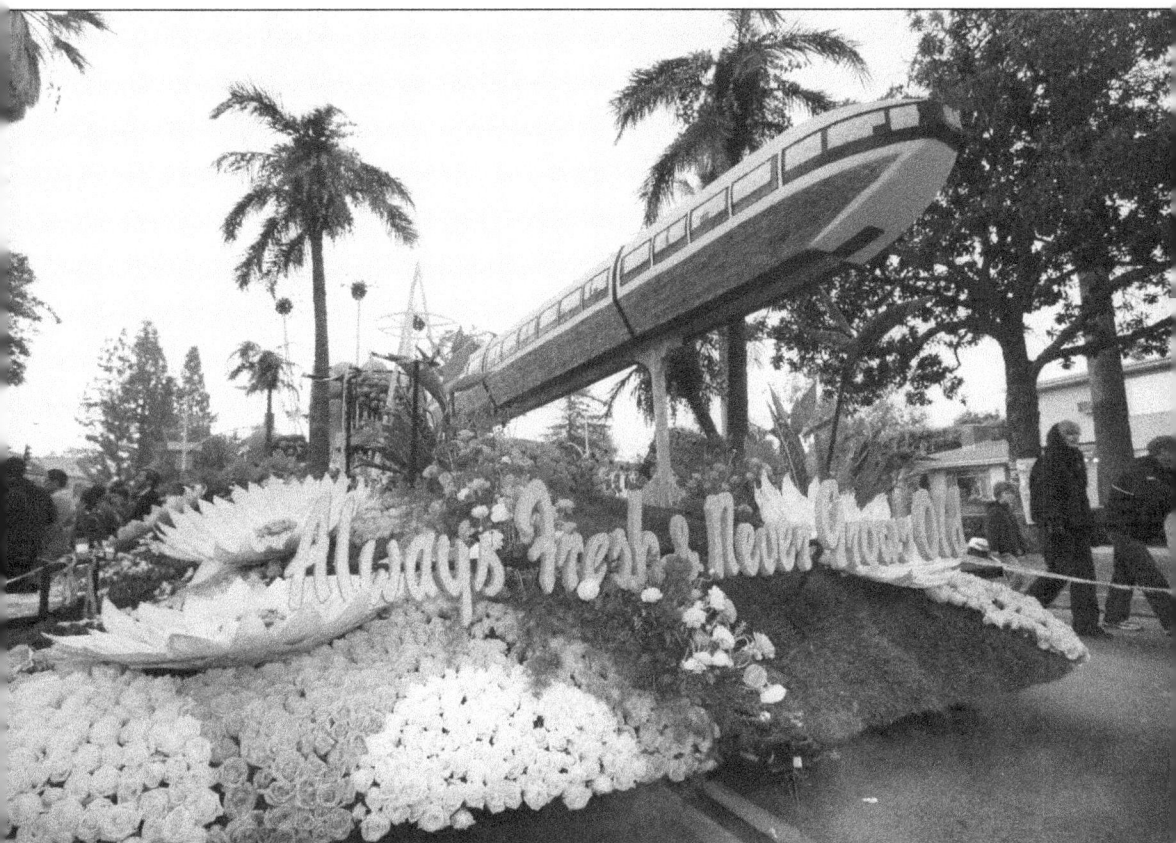

After a wait of 36 years, Anaheim again offered a float for the 2007 Pasadena Tournament of Roses Parade. As part of Anaheim's 150th birthday celebration, the float included several Anaheim icons, including orange crates, palm trees, a river, the Disneyland Monorail, and of course, a small version of the 230-foot-tall "Big-A." *American Idol* finalist and Anaheim resident Lisa Tucker was joined by six students, winners of the mayor's TechScholar program, who rode the five-and-a-half-mile route. As was the case over three decades earlier, Anaheim's 55-foot-long entry was an award winner, this time the coveted Mayor's Award. Anaheim, where things are "Always Fresh and Never Grow Old" coupled with its "can do" spirit has led it to become an international tourist destination and the state's 10th largest city as it begins its 150th year.

Visit us at
arcadiapublishing.com

www.ingramcontent.com/pod-product-compliance
Lightning Source LLC
Chambersburg PA
CBHW080548110426
42813CB00006B/1250